PRESENTED BY #1 BEST-SELLING AUTHOR

ANGELA R. EDWARDS

TEEN TALK

Embracing One's
Identity in Today's Times

TEEN TALK

Embracing One's Identity in Today's Times

Compiled By:
Angela R. Edwards

Young Adult Foreword By:
Christina Danielle Wilson

Teen Influencer Foreword By:
Pastor Rodney Bennett

Supporting Cast Members:
Aniyah Vital
Ariel Thomas
Elijah Hogan
Gracie Greene
John Oakes
La'Tajia Thompson
Shakeyra Williams
Shatoria Stanford
Tamya Hibbler
Tayler Wright-Williams

Pearly Gates Publishing, LLC, Houston, Texas

Teen Talk:
Embracing One's Identity in Today's Times

Print ISBN 13: 978-1-947445-03-1
Digital ISBN 13: 978-1-947445-87-1

Scripture references are used with permission from Zondervan via Biblegateway.com.
Public Domain.

For information and bulk ordering, contact:
Pearly Gates Publishing, LLC
Angela Edwards, CEO
P.O. Box 62287
Houston, TX 77205
BestSeller@PearlyGatesPublishing.com

Dedication

To every teenager who has faced
trials and chose to be
VICTORIOUS,
this book is for
YOU!

Acknowledgments

First and foremost, all glory, honor, and praise are given to our Heavenly Father. We thank Him for the *Teen Talk* vision and pray those who read this book come to see their life's purpose revealed.

To **Christina Danielle Wilson**: Thank you for agreeing to be a part of this project. The transparency of your Foreword as one who is "fresh out of the teen years" is truly remarkable! Glory to God for your testimony!

To **Pastor Rodney Bennett**: I am grateful for your readiness to sow words of encouragement into our youth. Your Foreword is fantastic and speaks very well of the teen experience! Thank you for not hesitating when asked to share your empowering words with our youth!

To each of the **Teen Contributors:** You are the ones who remained after the opportunity was presented. **YOU DID IT!** You are now officially authors! Thank you *ALL* for realizing your story has value and that your words have **POWER!** May God continue to bless you on your life's journey!

Young Adult Foreword

"Know yourself. Know your worth." ~ Drake

Growing. Up. Sucks. It doesn't get any better when you're done "growing up." Just when you think you're on your way to 'adulting,' trust me…you're not. *(I'm speaking from experience. I'm only 22 years old.)* You're in the weird, ***"I can do whatever I want 'cause I'm grown!"*** and ***"Dang, I still need my mama to pay for these shoes"*** phase. It's feeling as if you can do **ANYTHING**, but you're restricted from doing it.

Some of your friends are having babies with two full-time jobs, seemingly to have their lives already figured out. Some are going to college, and some aren't doing a thing…and then there's **you**.

So, no: I am not gonna do that thing where I tell you everything is going to be okay—where I tell you, *"All you must do is believe in yourself"* or *"Your time is coming."* I'm not gonna tell you that you gotta push a little bit longer. As young people, we hear those words so often that our minds become numb to them. They have turned into "things" that people say *(usually the ones who have all their sh... **STUFF** together).*

Well, a lot of the time, I truly feel like I am not together. Most of the time, I feel like I am a complete and utter mess! And because you're reading this book, you probably feel or have felt the same way. I tell you that because sometimes, it's easier to know that there's somebody who's practically just like you out there following their dreams, rather than thinking that once the age of 18 hits, you must be a superhero.

I started college in 2015 at Alabama State University. My experience there started out great and gradually turned into something I never thought would happen. Suddenly, there were people who hated me, grown men getting groups of girls together to fight me, and people telling me I didn't deserve life itself. It was tough! The toughest of all was when, in the Fall semester of 2017, I was raped. I kept it to myself for months. I became distant and found myself in a perpetual state of sadness – the type of despair where if God took me off the earth at that very moment, I wouldn't have cared.

I was pledging for a theatre organization on campus when it finally came out that the young "man" who had assaulted me violated two of my line sisters as well. That turned into an even bigger obstruction. People hated me for "lying," saying I was only searching for attention. *"Why would he rape* ***YOU****?"* they accusingly taunted. For the next two months, the assault was fresh all over again. *(I never crossed the organization, by the way.)* My mother immediately came to the school to get me, and I transferred to Georgia State University.

Okay. Let's fast forward two months to the very first time I ever saw myself on television. Yes, I went from depression to severely chasing my dreams by any means necessary. I went from literally not caring if I dropped off the face of the earth to being on set with people like Queen Latifah, Tiffany Haddish, and Kevin Hart! I received my first leading role in a college stage play, released my first poetry ep, and began designing my own clothing line.

Fast forward again.

I graduated college, got an amazing job with a traveling theatre, became the Assistant Director of an academy, acquired an agent, and am **STILL** chasing my dreams with everything I have. No, I don't have it all together. I'm still diligently searching for new ways to follow my dreams every single day. What I want you to gain from my story is that what would typically take years to do, God can do in a matter of months, hours, or heck, **SECONDS** if He really wanted to show you who He is!

GOD can heal you in minutes!

GOD can give you the breakthrough you need in minutes!

GOD can get you the job you want without any qualifications in minutes!

GOD CAN DO IT ALL!

Reading self-help books and watching some of the people I look up to, like Devon Franklin, Meghan Goode, Denzel Washington, and Viola Davis (to name a few) every day, helped me to keep going and inspired me in so many ways. A lot of times, I had to turn off the phone, TV, and music, literally stand in front of the mirror, and cry before God. I saw all the yuck and disgusting parts of me, things about myself I really didn't want to see. And yes, I'm still in the process.

Sometimes, isolating yourself from the world is the best way to conquer it.

Sometimes, you gotta lose friends because they can't go where God is taking you—and that's okay!

Sometimes, you can't go to every party—and that's okay!

Sometimes *(well, a lot of times)*, when you're destined for greatness, you must walk with just God and you in faith so that He can show you what's next—and that's okay, too!

One of my favorite quotes ever that a professor said to me was, *"Christina, you can't wanna do what everybody else does and be different at the same time."* I have been riding the wave of my differences ever since!

So, **NOW** is the part where I tell you:

- Believe in yourself because if you don't find the strength to love who you are and the gifts that God gave you, you will never, ever be happy.
- Once you figure out that God and you are one and that **ALL** things happen for the good of those who love the Lord,

nothing—no matter how bad—will ever keep you down.

- Keep pushing; your time is coming. It may not come in the way you expect it, but the blessing is there. Keep pushing!
- Don't let your mind become numb to the motivation and inspiration God has set up all around you in your walk of life. It means something.
- You gotta be so secure in yourself that Satan himself can walk in your room, and you can look past him like he ain't even there!

Have no fear. Do not resist the process. Have faith that who God created you to be is more than enough to accomplish what He has planned for you. I'm still making my way to the fulfillment of my dreams. As we make this journey together and embark on our separate paths to success, keep the words of this book—every story and every truth—in mind. You're gonna need it!

Christina Danielle Wilson

Founder, TwelveTwoProductions

YouTube: Tina Not Turner

Instagram/Twitter: _TinaNotTurner

Teen Influencer Foreword

#YallGotNext

When a team plays a good game and is victorious over their opponent, they have a way of bragging about their win while calling out their next "victim" *(or so they think)*. The winners look around, and someone will usually scream ***"Who got next?"*** to the next team ready for battle.

As adults, we have played many quarters in the game of life…but life is not a game. Personally, I am shifting my energy to coach today's youth to prepare them for what's to come because it is their time now: **THEY GOT NEXT!**

Let me introduce myself.

I am "RB Platinum," aka Rodney Bennett, aka Rev. Rodney. I am a youth motivational speaker, former athlete, and soon-to-be Bestselling Author. As one of the world's leading authorities on overcoming adversity and rebuilding hope, I am also the Dean of a new learning institution called The University of

Adversity. Several years ago, I looked back over my life and the experiences I overcame and said to myself, *"The one thing I can easily give to anyone is hope."* At that time, Platinum Hope was born. Unlike regular hope that is likened to dreaming or wishing, the platinum version is an upgrade. Platinum Hope is a strong, fortified desire that is superglued to a bold—almost arrogant—expectation of attaining a goal.

Among today's youth, the pressure to quit due to feelings of hopelessness has increased dramatically, so why not increase their reasons not to? There is a need for new hope! Sadly, the number one cause of suicide is hopelessness. Statistics show that suicide is the second leading cause of death among 10- to 24-year-olds. Additionally, every day in the U.S., there are over 3,000 suicide *attempts* among 9th to 12th graders. **Wow!** I am convinced that teens and young adults will benefit from a new way of thinking that upgrades their hope. **Hope is *DOPE*!**

At this point, you're probably thinking, *"Why is this dude so big on hope? What makes him think he can easily give it to somebody else?"* Good questions, my friend!

As a young man, between the ages of 10 and 24, I wrestled with eight of the deadliest assassins in the world. Those hired killers were introduced to me to murder my hopes, dreams, and calling, but they failed.

- At the age of ten, I was sexually abused by a non-family member.
- By age 11, I was already using nicotine.
- At the age of 13, I was drinking alcohol.
- By age 14, I was smoking marijuana… ***heavily***.
- I was only 15 when I fell in love with the "nightlife," aka the streets and club scenes. (SMH!)
- At age 16, I started using cocaine.
- By age 17, I was a street hustler (drug dealer) and became very promiscuous.
- By the time I was 23, I was known as "Rock," "Rocky Balboa," and "Rockstar," and had become a full-blown drug addict.

By the grace of God, I walked away from those assassins almost 20 years ago. It was a war, but I am free, healed, and whole through the blood of Jesus and a praying Momma! I have decided to make my life an open book so that I can help young people successfully pass the exams of life.

Somewhere around the age of 12, I really started to appreciate the game of football. That year, my dad bought me a set of weights for Christmas, and it was on! As I look back today, I can clearly see **that** was when I began to develop a solid identity. I started learning about football and talking about playing the sport. As time progressed and I observed myself playing the game, I realized I was good—and so did many others around me. I began to tell myself, *"One day, I'm going to play pro football!"* Many (but not all) others agreed with me. I was on my way!

This is who I **became**: A college graduate, professional athlete, family man, and one who played a vital role in building the family business in transportation.

The interesting thing is that it was during that time when the assassins located me. Let me be clear here: As the negative, destructive influences began to close in on my life, I had to make a critical decision. **Which identity was I going to choose?**

I remember growing up and attending Burlington Township Middle School in Burlington, New Jersey. There was a guidance counselor there named Mrs. Bolling. She was awesome! She helped me to make the correct scholastic decisions that would lead me to my desired career goal. At the same time, I had another influencer called "Mr. Popularity." People—both young and old—were beginning to know my name. Some young people were drawn to me who were not the right kind of influences. My mother would often say, *"Boy, it's the company you keep!"* I would always respond, *"Mom, I don't have any peer pressure!"* When I acted wiser than I actually was, my mom had a nickname she would use for me that was most befitting: **"Simpleton."**

Like clockwork, by the time I was in my second year of high school, peer pressure, growing popularity, and the persistence and skill of those hired assassins ("Dream Killers") guided me into making some horrible decisions. Somewhere along the way, I had misplaced my identity.

I recall around that time, I went to a lot of parties *(unless, of course, I was on punishment or "restriction," as my parents called it)*. I also remember one time thinking, *"Man, I'm 14 years old! Ain't I grown enough to make my own decisions?!"* Just then, I looked out the window and saw my dad getting into his taxicab to head out to work and thought, *"Nope. I'll just go read a magazine."* I wasn't as grown as I thought! The height of my youth shame during my "coolness career" in my high school years had to be when my homeboys came to pick me up, and my mother intercepted the ringing doorbell while I stood astonished in the background. *"No, Rodney is not going anywhere today.* ***He's on punishment****!"* My boys walked away in disbelief, cracking up all the while.

There was another time not long after that when I planned on going to another party with some friends. For some reason, at the last minute, I didn't feel like going (which, even to me, was strange). The next day, someone asked me if I heard what happened the night before. When I said I hadn't, they went on to explain the following:

"Someone was driving a vehicle late last night, coming from a party, when they lost control. The car slid right under a tractor-trailer, shearing off the roof as if it had been done with a large can opener. When

that happened, the front seat passenger could not escape, and he was instantly decapitated."

I later learned that after I declined to go to the party, my friend looked for and found a replacement rider. Then, it hit me like a ton of bricks: **That bloody, mangled seat is where I would have been had I gone to the party!** Just the thought still gives me chills to this day. Almighty God had intervened in an unwise decision I could have gotten myself into. I almost made a choice that would have permanently changed my identity, my life, and the lives of those who loved me.

Admittedly, my friends and I never realized when we were teenagers that **WE HAD NEXT!** ***WE*** were going to be the game-changers of tomorrow! However, because of our lifestyles, some of us missed many opportunities to make a difference in our communities, our cultures, our families, and even our nation back then. We would likely have permanently forfeited our impact, as well as the miracle of being rerouted to our true identity, were it not for a small army of prayer warriors who refused to give up on us.

Fast forward…

Today, many of us *(my friends and I)* are business owners, great parents, schoolteachers, lawyers, ministers, and even judges!

Young people, it is as much ***(if not more)*** of a priority for you to today grip your identity as it is playing your next game of Super Smash Bros, Black Ops 2, or Zelda *(yes, I said it)*! Those games are fun and maybe even addictive on some level, but they will have no impact on your destiny. This current generation will need all your gifts and talents tomorrow, including me! Remember: **YOU GOT NEXT!**

Your identity is awesome because you are **UNIQUE**! Through intelligent design, nothing in this world is identical—not even identical twins. That means you are a designer's original masterpiece! There is ***no one*** on the whole planet earth just like you. That means you will look different, sound different, learn differently, and create differently.

One of the pillars or 'I Core' attitudes I discuss as a youth speaker is "I-Cope." Basically, it addresses how you deal with things. Let me ask: How do ***YOU*** cope? Have no doubt about it: The adversities and conflicts of today's times are more intense, more violent, and more stressful than they have ever been. Young people, this is **YOUR** world now. I heard a teacher recently share how they must train elementary school children on what to do in case of an active shooter. That's sad but necessary. When I was a child, we had something called a 'bomb drill.' We went into the hallway and kneeled for about 60 seconds as if there were a bomb outside, but there never was.

Sometimes, it almost seems as if the people we entrust to address national issues have somehow disconnected from the real problems our society faces today. This world has changed. In response, the way we solve and cope with difficulties must also change. That is why it is so awesome to be unique! Your uniqueness will adapt to the problems that need to be solved today. Your identity will help identify the challenges of your generation like nobody else because you are uniquely qualified to do so! The uniqueness of your character is the bombdotcom! (I don't know if y'all still say that. I stay current with the "cool language" of today as I listen to my two daughters. Then, I'll say something like, *"Ayo! What's poppin'?"* and one of them will say,

"I can't with you!" while the other says, *"I love it when you talk hip!"* That's **not** flattering. LOL!)

I remember talking to a youth group I was leading a couple of years ago in Washington, DC. I was trying to develop a way to ignite a fire in them to want to change on their own. After racking my 40-something-year-old brain for about two weeks, I came up empty. Finally, I had a lightbulb or "DUH!" moment: **Why not just ask them?** So, I did a survey that asked them, *"What three things are needed for you to grow?"* Overwhelmingly, their responses came in the following order:

1. Read the Bible more.
2. Learn how to pray and do it more consistently.
3. Walk away from the wrong friends.

I was blown away! The audience consisted of a mixed group of roughly 30 people, ranging in age from 10 to 22 years old! They were more in tune with what they needed than I thought, likely because they were uniquely closer to their issues than I was. Young people, you are closer to understanding your problems than you think you are. Listen to yourself sometimes *(but not **ALL** the time)*! LOL!

The world is becoming more and more diverse as time goes by. There are more and more perspectives that must come together. Diversity and inclusion are, unfortunately, significant challenges in today's society. They are also why we must grasp our identities. We are all a piece of the puzzle, especially teens. Sometimes, we (older people) are guilty of judging our youth without even attempting to get to know them. It's so easy for me—as "Generation X" and an African American male—to look at a young man walking down the street with his pants sagging and think, *"That doesn't look good. I just don't understand!"* That begs the question: **Have I ever really tried to?** Most times, the answer is no. That must change if we are going to thrive (not just survive) together. We must at least try to understand those who are not like us—young and old, black and white, rich and poor—because we cannot change the trends of our population. They don't stand still or go in reverse, as some would like to see. Sorry. It's not going to happen. Time only goes forward, so we might as well put down our gavels, stop judging, and start listening.

It is important to realize that my individual identity is not a threat to yours.

Instead, it complements it when we draw strength from our differences and learn how to play together based on those differences. Think about it: That is what championship teams do, such as the Pittsburgh Steelers (sorry; had to throw my favorite football team in here)! Exceptional teams learn to play well off each other's strengths and weaknesses. Our individual identities are necessary to embrace so that we can win together!

In the neighborhood I grew up in, we all pretty much got along. There were, however, always exceptions to the racial diversity presented. I would ask that you be careful not to let another generation (your elders) transfer their racial bias onto you. You can respectfully listen to someone, but that doesn't mean you must agree with everything they say. Just as theirs are, your identity is unique to your culture and history. One generation's identity does not have to match another's in every way. In fact, it cannot. I find it interesting that it's as if the younger generations seem more tolerant and accepting of others' identities than generations past. It's just a personal observation, but our youth seem more at peace with the shift in diversity while appreciating their own uniqueness in the process. Great job, young people! Keep up the good work!

To the older people, I say, ***"Learn from them!"***

On a personal level, I can look back at my life and realize I searched for many things while trying to find fulfillment. When you have not embraced your identity, you will always be searching for the "wrong" thing, not realizing it until you acquire the "right" thing. For years during my addiction to drugs and alcohol, I was on a quest to find the next best feeling. Much of that was because of the unsettled, wounded feelings I tried to escape. There were some drugs I never tried—by the grace of God. I remember when I lived in a city many years ago that was far from home. I never indulged in heroin, but somehow, at one point in my life, there were some people around me who did. In that city, there was a sudden rash of overdoses. At least two of my friends died during that time. Others I knew were so far detached from their identity that they identified with death more easily than life. When those overdoses occurred, there was a rush of people who tried to find the drug that took away life, just so they could try it!

Today, I am also a drug and alcohol counselor. Much of what I do is helping people on different levels connect with their true identity without drugs and with God. I believe there **IS** a cure.

Young people, it is wise to listen to your parents, family, and loved ones when they are telling you what they think is best for you. That may involve a particular school or college, hairstyle, piercings, a financial matter, a car, or something else you want. And yes, it most certainly may pertain to a boyfriend or girlfriend. Your loved ones care about you, so they want what they feel is in your best interest. You should respect that while, at the same time, still embrace your own identity. It's also okay to rock your identity when you are expressing your individuality. As you grow and mature, learn how to articulate what your unique desires and preferences are and why. People will listen to you more readily when you can communicate clearly and respectfully. Be okay with agreeing to disagree with people as well. Sometimes, it's not a matter of being right or wrong; it's just "different."

When you appreciate your identity, you must sometimes fight for it, but the payoff is worth it. Many times, when you accept things others choose for you, it may be useful, but, on some level, it may leave you unfulfilled. That's why it's important to take time and really get to know yourself. Only then will you find out what it is you really want. Many adults have waited to chase their dreams. Why did that happen? The answer is simple: Because they settled.

I would venture to say as you get halfway through high school, you should have some idea of who you are, who you want to become, and why. Where your identity and purpose are determined is where you will find fulfillment and satisfaction. Some people want others to feel more satisfied than they do themselves, basically camouflaging their identity. Eventually, the truth of who they are will surface. When it does, however, it may come with a feeling of regret. You do **NOT** want to arrive at a place later in life with major regrets (some minor ones are often unavoidable and easier to live with; that's a part of our humanness).

It's also vital that you embrace your identity in today's times because you are in for a change. This world is always discovering something "new," from diet, to careers, to solar systems, and computer games. With time, your identity will evolve as well. It's okay; let it. Some places in your life will remain blank for now. Relax. Those blanks will fill in over time. There will be some foods you hate today that you may come to love five years from now, like okra or liver. As an example, today, I love a genre of music that I thought was the most boring, tortuous thing to listen to when I was young: classical. Give yourself permission to change and grow!

Before I go, let me share something with you. For many years, my life was very dark. There were times when, even as a young person, I didn't want to get up and face another day. I was very close to becoming hopeless. Even during the beginning years of being a changed person, the files of old replayed in my head. The past was no longer my present, yet it continually talked to me as if it were. The voices in my head would say, *"The person you used to be is the person you still are"*—which I knew was not true. But because of so much hurt and pain I caused my parents, family, and friends (not to mention myself), that gnawing feeling remained and told me I was worthless.

Let me tell you something about **TODAY**: If I could package myself—my gifts, calling, personality, etc.—in a box and put it in a store in a locked showcase, guess what? Only the top 1% of the world's population would be able to afford it! One primary reason my self-worth is off the chain is that I am **NOW** walking in my true identity…and all of you will, too! **Y'ALL GOT NEXT!**

Pastor Rodney Bennett

www.rbplatinum.com
Facebook: The University of Adversity
Email: platinumhope2@gmail.com

Preface

At the time this book is published, I will soon celebrate *(Lord willing)* being on this earth for half a century ***(yes, 50 years)***—which means I left my teens a **LONG, LONG** time ago. However, the memories of my teenage years seem to pop up randomly. Some make me smile, while others make me cringe. I have no doubt if you sat with your parent/caretaker and discussed **THEIR** youth *(something I encourage)*, you would find you have more in common than you think! I am almost 50 years old and blessed to still talk with my 75-year-old mother about her teen years. I find myself in awe at the similarities in the lives we have both lived.

Recently, my best friend and I recalled the moment we entered our 8th-grade talent show. We, along with two other friends, chose to portray the Mary Jane Girls *(an 80's R&B all-girl group)*. Let me just pause and ask: **How awesome is it that my bestie and I have been friends for almost 45 years?!** Okay. Okay. Back to the point. The talent show was a very fond memory. As best we could, we dressed like the women on the album cover, watched their videos to learn their style of dance, and then, on the day of the show, we **NAILED IT**…but we ***LOST*** to a boy I will call "Danny Boy" who showed up and had the audience roaring with laughter at his comedic stylings. My friends and I couldn't believe it! We worked **SO** hard, perfecting our lip-syncing routine…and we ***LOST!*** Teen devastation is saying it mildly. Somehow, we managed to get past the disappointment. *(It helped to hear from a countless number of our peers that we* ***SHOULD*** *have won.)*

There's another time I recall when I was peer pressured into bullying a girl who was clearly no threat to me whatsoever. With my "friends" cheering me on to ask the girl for one of her Twinkies during lunch, I approached her. As I took every step, everything in me screamed, ***"LEAVE HER ALONE! THIS ISN'T RIGHT!"*** Did that voice stop my feet from moving? No. So, when I asked her for that tasty treat and was denied, I punched her in the face and **TOOK** not one, but ***BOTH*** Twinkies. That brought on a slew of laughter from my "friends," and I—not them—was suspended from school.

Here's the thing: I didn't know then like I now know that for every action, there's an opposite and even stronger **REACTION**. I had to pay the price for what I did to that girl.

That punishment came during my sophomore year in high school. I found myself being bullied by a neighbor of mine. I was close friends with her sister *(and still am)*, but the bully hung out with a totally different set of people *(they were **all** bullies)*. While in school one day, people kept coming up to me, telling me the girl wanted to fight me. It must be noted that we were neighbors, so we rode the bus to and from school together every day. I had **NO** idea what was coming. I tried to talk to her to find out if the rumors were true. *"What did I do that makes you want to fight **ME**?!"* I asked. She turned around and walked away, but not before giving me the middle finger. That day, we rode the bus home, and it was eerily quiet. As soon as we got off at our stop, the girl approached me and mentioned something about what I supposedly said to her stepfather about her and her boyfriend *(the account of what I actually said was totally **TWISTED**, which explained why she was so angry)*. Guess what happened next? You guessed correctly if you said, *"She punched you in the face."* That was the end of the confrontation. I refused to fight her, so I walked away with tears streaming down my face. As I made my way home, that same voice I heard in 8th grade whispered, *"I told you to leave that girl alone. You had to answer for what you did to her."* **OUCH!**

The moral of the story is this: the adults in your life and I understand the plights of your teenage years. Many of the things you will encounter along your teen journey are not new, just different.

"What has been will be again, what has been done will be done again; there is nothing new under the sun" **(Ecclesiastes 1:9).**

Did you catch that? There is **NOTHING** new under the sun. **NOT. A. THING.**

As you walk your unique path on this thing called "LIFE," know that you will find your way. Don't give up just because you had a moment *(or a lot of moments)* where you feel alone and as if no one understands what you're going through. It is likely that talking about "it" with your peers won't help much because it is likely they are enduring their own set of challenges.

Now, I'm **NOT** saying don't talk to them about whatever issues you are having. What I ***AM*** saying is seek out support from an adult you trust—one who will listen, has been there and done that, and can help guide you through to the other side.

We all stumble and fall. Even as adults, we make mistakes for which we must be held accountable. Be grateful for the real friendships you make along the way. Lean on and embrace them in times of trouble. You are **NOT** alone! Allow your spirit to direct you to the person who will have your best interest at heart so that you can release the mess that the enemy of your soul—Satan—uses to keep you bound *(i.e., depressed, brokenhearted, lonely, suicidal, etc.)*.

This is your life, and you only have one. Live your life with purpose! If you need a reason to fight your way out of your youth, try this on for size:

SOMEONE is going to one day need **YOU** to encourage them! **YOU** can be the voice of reason and hope!

Introduction

"There is a season (a time appointed) for everything, and a time for every delight and event or purpose under Heaven…a time to weep and a time to laugh, a time to mourn and a time to dance"
(Ecclesiastes 3: 1,4).

Just when you think you're all alone and that no one can empathize with what you're going through, here comes a book filled with true stories written by teens for teens! Virtually every hardship teenagers go through is discussed on the pages of *Teen Talk: Embracing One's Identity in Today's Times.* Undoubtedly, there is something unique about your life that you would tell differently; however, the individuals who shared their overcoming stories are sure to empower you to survive another day…and the day after that…and so on.

Teen Talk is a product of the need to give teens a voice to their deepest concerns. Each contributor (*referred to as a "Supporting Cast Member")* tells their story in a way that only they can. They have poured out their hearts, which allowed the healing process to begin for many of them. Words have power, and with each one penned on the pages of this book, you are sure to connect with at least one Supporting Cast Member's truth.

Bullying? It's in here.

Struggling with academics? It's in here.

Promiscuity? It's in here.

Suicide attempts? It's in here.

But wait! Although teens wrote this book from their viewpoint, parents and caretakers are encouraged to read it as well. It may seem as if it's been eons ago that your parents, grandparents, aunts, and uncles were teenagers, but rest assured they can also relate to the stories written here. Truth be told, many of your elders may still experience issues with embracing their identities—and that's okay! As humans, our lives are always changing due to one circumstance or another. It is in that space you are asked to spend time speaking with those who have already gone through trials similar to your own. If they are honest with you, you will see that no matter the age, the memories of days gone by will float to the surface, allowing you to connect on a deeper level. As adults, we do not want you to think we "don't understand." We do. We ***REALLY*** do….more than you realize.

So, as you turn page after page, reading story after story, begin to think of how you can approach someone to talk about whatever is causing you internal torment. Holding things inside is not only stressful and can lead to anxiety and depression; it's also physically unhealthy to do so. Stress can lead to headaches, muscle tension, chest pains, and so much more *(yes, young people can also suffer from those adult-like ailments).* Come out from behind the four walls of your bedroom and spend time talking with the adults in your life. They need to know what's happening in your life so that they can help you. If you're maintaining a "fake smile," how can anyone know there's something deep down inside that's bothering you?

Use the power of **YOUR** words to effect change in your life. Speak up and speak out! I repeat: **YOU ARE NOT ALONE! SPEAK UP!**

Table of Contents

Supporting Cast Member
Aniyah Vital

Aniyah Vital is a 9th-grader in CCISD. Aniyah is in a blended family. She is the second oldest of four girls to her dad and the youngest of two girls by her mom. Aniyah loves anime, and she has a passion for art. Upon completion of high school, she would like to attend an HBCU to major in Art. Aniyah can be very goofy, and she's a jokester. She displays loads of sarcasm but is genuinely a caring person. She enjoys music of different varieties, which fosters her love for dancing. Aniyah is more introverted than extroverted and values her alone/quiet time.

I AM NO LONGER "THAT GIRL"

At one point in time, I wanted to kill myself. Yeah. I did. It's kind of weird saying it so straightforwardly. I was a depressed girl who covered my sadness with a smile. I felt as if nobody cared about me and that I was a failure to my family. I then converted my sadness into doing something "productive": I used to punch and sometimes cut myself. I shouldn't have done those things, though. Self-harm is never a good outlet.

I suppose I should explain what caused my sadness and self-hatred so severely…

The first main issue was that my family separated. Now, that may not sound so tragic to some, but it was hard on my older sister, Iyana, and me. My parents were both young when they had my sister and me, and it was hard for them to take care of us. Money was tight, and it was difficult for them to keep jobs, making it hard for us to survive in such a cruel world. As Iyana and I got older, and our parents started to drift apart *(once we were old enough)*, they finally parted ways.

Our mother took us with her and cared for us…to a certain degree.

Honestly, our mother wasn't really the problem. She is sweet, but some of her boyfriends used to be mean to us. I can only really remember one of her boyfriends abusing our mother. He used to punch and kick her for no reason, and he would whoop us for the smallest things. Even though he took care of us by buying essential items and keeping a roof over our heads, I was always scared he would harm us again. That same man's son also did something cruel to me: he molested me. He only violated me once, but that moment is still engraved in my mind. He used to touch my body in weird ways. I was scared but didn't tell anyone because I thought I would get in trouble if I told what he did to me. *Plus, I didn't think anyone would help me, so I kept it to myself.*

Our mother also moved to different locations, trying to get away from her crazy exes. After the horrendous actions her boyfriend inflicted upon us, our father took her to court and fought for custody of my sister and me—and he won, giving our mother the time to change herself for both our sake and her health. Today, she is a woman of truth. She is married to a faithful man, she visits us frequently, and she does her best not to leave us out of her life. She's happier than she has ever been, and it makes me so glad to see her achieve her dreams. I'm so glad she changed her life for her own wellbeing.

After Iyana and I started living with our father full time, lots of things changed about me. I began to learn more about myself and who I wanted to be. I embraced the different lessons my sisters and father taught me and was proud to be who I was at that point. In a word, I was **HAPPY**. I was also glad to have someone around my age to talk to and who understood my point of view. I felt safe in the comfort of my father's home. I was happy to be loved and happy to be cherished for being who I wanted to be. *(It must be noted that I was loved and cherished by both parents, but in different ways.)* Good things happened all around me, and I was cheerful. My father finally got his business up and running, and everyone was doing well in school. We were all joyful about the direction our lives were headed.

Everything was great, until our mother stopped coming to pick up Iyana and me to spend time with her. I didn't know what was wrong; she just suddenly stopped coming to get us for our usual visits. The weekends we didn't get to see her made me severely angry and sad. *Did she not want to see us? Or was she going through something and didn't want to tell us?* I became sad…depressed, even. I couldn't help but be upset about my mother's abrupt exit from my life. I would stay in my room most of the time. I didn't want to face the world or accept that my mother wasn't going to come to see Iyana and me.

As a result of my ever-growing despair, I tried to kill myself. I was in 5th grade at the time. That first time, I nervously slit my wrist and *(obviously)* was unsuccessful. Over time, I started to cut lightly into my arm, leaving little marks. I wasn't happy about cutting myself. It didn't feel good, and there was always a lot of blood, even when I would cut myself only a little bit. I remember the time Iyana caught me. It was so awkward. She was going to tell on me, but I begged her not to because I was scared I would get in trouble. She said if I stopped cutting myself, she wouldn't tell. So, I tried to stop.

Around the same time, when I finally decided I couldn't take it anymore, I wanted to leave all the hurt behind me. Hurting myself wasn't enough; I wanted to end my life. My mother wasn't coming to get us, my stepmother's mother passed away, and I was getting "lowkey bullied." **I was fed up!** I could no longer take all the negativity, all the rude comments, and all the pain anymore. I then tried conveying my pain in picture form, displaying my hurt in my artwork. That caught the teacher's attention, and the principal was notified. The principal asked me about how I was feeling and if I needed help. I refused to talk about my issues with her, so she called my parents. She explained to them that I needed to be checked into a mental hospital and would have to be evaluated by the doctor that was there as well. My parents did what they had to do to get me back into school, so they took me to the hospital.

I was a resident in the hospital for three days—and hated every minute. The food was disgusting, and the adults in the facility were ill-mannered. I met lots of kids who were just like me, all with different stories about how and why they were there. For example, one of the boys was there because he killed his animal companion, then laughed about it.

As you can probably tell by now, I didn't ***really*** belong there, but there was a lesson learned from what I saw and experienced. I won't tell you about the lesson right now. I will, however, tell you after I explain what happened in therapy, how I learned to resolve my suicidal tendencies, and how I can help you fix yours.

Anyway, back to my story…

There was a strict protocol that was followed every day: The inmates and I would wake up extremely early to eat breakfast in a room that was relatively empty (it wasn't really a room; it was more like a random open space in our section of the building that had a small plastic table). We would then sit at the table with a counselor who would ask the same questions, such as, *"How do you feel today?"* and *"Do you feel like hurting yourself?"* Every single day, I would respond that I was fine and wanted to go home. Of course, they wouldn't allow me to go home until I was cleared to do so by the doctor. We had to keep the door open to our rooms, and I can't forget to mention the bathroom didn't have a door whatsoever. We all had to take showers and eat dinner at the same time, too. The shower arrangements were the **worst**! They had no curtains, which I could understand (somebody could've hung themselves with them), and the water was ***cold***! *(At least provide us with some hot water if you're going to keep us locked away!)*

On the third day, my parents came to get me. I was **SO** happy to get out of that nightmarish situation!

Afterward, my parents grew close again and started to collaborate more than ever before. Things began to take an extremely good turn. Everyone seemed happy, and we all started therapy (my father and his wife, as well as my mother).

My mother got into a new religion, and she became different. She was happier, lively, and loved her life and how it was changing. Iyana and I were the ones who witnessed her change. She stopped dating bad men and changed her mannerisms and some bad habits that had blinded her. My sister and I went along with her transformation and did whatever she asked of us (if it had something to do with her religion). After some time, my sister got tired of feeling brainwashed and no longer wanted to go along with our mother's faith, so she talked to her about it. Of course, our mother didn't agree with what my sister said. Being the person I am, I still went along with it because I didn't want to lose her again.

Well, it wasn't long before it happened…***again***. Our mother didn't come to get us for about six to seven months.

I was devastated! My depression got worse, making it hard for me to function. I knew she had disappeared because we didn't truly agree with her religion. A loving mother would have accepted that we didn't agree with all the material that was presented to us, but **OUR** mother took the "easy route." She left, just as she always did when something bad happened or when things didn't go her way. Then, whenever she decided to return—weeks or months later—she tried to fix what she messed up.

I tried and tried to get our mother to come see and spend time with us, but she wouldn't. After about three months, I no longer cared about her absence from our lives. For those few months that our mother wasn't there, our aunty would pick up Iyana and me. She supported us, listened to our feelings, and empathized with how much pain our mother had mentally inflicted upon us. I will always be grateful that she was there during that difficult time. When our mother heard about how bad she had hurt us, she changed and came back. Obviously, I was mad and torn. I couldn't believe she thought she could walk in and out of our lives as much as she pleased! *(In time, I learned that was my reality and came to accept it.)*

Having depression can trigger other mental disorders, such as anxiety. I suffer from that condition, and it is difficult. I hyperventilate, and it's harsh on my body. It's hard to return to "normal" after dealing with anxiety. It was during those times when I would hurt myself (I don't do that anymore, though). One of the things I've learned to do so that I don't become overwhelmed is to take breaks between projects. It's a huge help!

Self-esteem was also something I couldn't easily grasp. It was complicated for me to understand. I didn't know how to love or cherish myself. Training to love me was as difficult as it sounds. Teaching myself to love what my skin looked like or how my personality was different from everybody else's was a chore. Self-esteem is something I'm still learning to do to this day, but as time goes by and I mature, I believe I will learn how to obtain confidence (have good self-esteem). Confidence is something someone with depression doesn't really possess. I can attest to that. I doubted myself and everything I did. Now that I've grown into and accepted who I am, I love myself and am glad I'm becoming the person I've always wanted to be.

Oh! I can't forget to give you the moral of my story!

The moral is that healing takes time. You must be patient during the process. Trying to get better quickly or sugarcoating the pain won't work. Talking to someone and putting your heart out there is super important to aid in developing a cleaner, non-suicidal mindset. Discussing your issues with people you trust—parents, friends (non-toxic ones), coworkers, or a therapist—is ideal. Most likely, they will try to help change your perception of your life. I, for one, know that changing is hard and the process is painfully slow, but you must persevere through the sorrow.

Expressing yourself is extremely essential to become mentally stable. Drawing, writing, exploring, and dancing are some examples that can help you express yourself and reflect on how you feel. Trying your best to become better should be your **priority**. Put more effort into becoming who you **want** to be, not what others ***expect*** you to be. It's also critical to change the way you look at yourself. For example, affirm yourself daily by repeating the following:

- **I AM WORTHY.**
- **I AM LOVED.**
- **I WILL CHANGE FOR THE BETTER.**

I know it may be challenging to see yourself as other than useless at times, but you must learn to accept who you are. When I couldn't and wouldn't do those things for myself, I tried to change the way I was expected to be in society until I learned to love the skin I'm in.

I appreciate every single person who helped and guided me to become the young woman I am today. I thank my parents, my family, and my therapist for their constant support during those daring, dark times in my life. I am grateful for the woman who let me submit this story for you to read. Last but not least, I thank **YOU** for reading about my life that has been both sad and loving. I'm thrilled that others finally get to know how my life has done a turnaround for the better! I am no longer **"THAT GIRL"**!

Supporting Cast Member
Ariel Thomas

Ariel Thomas is a Youth Worship Leader, Dancer, Writer, Traveler, and YouTuber. Most importantly, she loves being a Big Sis and friend to many. She helps her little sister with homeschool work, and when she is scared, Ariel comforts her. When with her friends, she laughs and sheds tears with them. When she isn't singing and speaking, she enjoys leading small groups of children into the knowledge and understanding of a relationship with Jesus Christ. Servant Leader would be the best way to describe the effortless giving from her heart. Ariel met Jesus at a young age and fell in love with Him.

IT'S ALL A PART OF GROWING UP

There's a lot that comes with not knowing your identity. It can cause you to be someone you're not or act outside yourself. You may even find that you are trying to impress some people who either like you as you are and don't care about how "uncool" you are *(or think you are)* **OR** others who constantly put you down and tell you that you aren't good enough. ***Frankly, if they treat you like the latter, they aren't worth your time.***

Along the way, you can lose some pretty great relationships, mainly because the people who genuinely like you won't appreciate the new person you're trying to become, and the people you're trying to impress who don't really care about you will never be happy with who you are. I know what it's like to feel you're not good enough. You may think, *"Hey, she's the girl behind the pen, so she must know all the answers."* Trust me; it's not like that at all. I've done some pretty dumb stuff to get the approval of my peers. The one dumb thing I did that I'm going to tell you about right now might be the ***dumbest*** of them all.

My family and I travel full-time in a travel trailer *(basically, we are on a two-year road trip).* We visit places all over the country and the world. When we first got our trailer, it was old and needed to be fixed up, so we stayed in our hometown for a couple of months while my parents made the necessary repairs.

When I first found out we were leaving, I was pretty upset *(to say the least).* I **hated** the idea and thought it was super lame. To add the massive cherry on top, I had to tell all my best friends who I'd known since the second grade that I was leaving. For what, anyway? To ***TRAVEL***? *(Crazy, I know. Traveling the world would be a dream come true for many people, but anger caused me to put on blinders. I couldn't see past my own pride.)* Making that announcement was weird. I wasn't exactly seen as "cool" by my peers, yet there I was, forced to make a wacko announcement that I was moving from place to place. That wouldn't do at all. I had to be better than that. ***I had to be "cool."*** For once, I needed a cover story, and just like that, I became **"Ariel: The girl moving to Hollywood to become an actress and pursue her career."** It was the "perfect lie," snappy *and* cool!

Everybody was super excited for me. They kept telling me how happy they were for me and, for a while, I almost cracked and told them the truth—but then, when some girls who weren't always kind to me tried to befriend me, I forgot all about exposing the truth.

NOTE: If someone *SUDDENLY* starts being nice to you because you're acting like a totally different person, they **PROBABLY** don't actually like you.

So, the months passed, and I maintained the lie—so much so that I started to believe it myself! I was determined to make sure **everyone** knew just how awesome I was. *(I'll let you in on a little secret: Lies hurt a lot, not only to the people you lied to but yourself as well.)* The truth was that the trip wasn't as bad as I initially thought. As a matter of fact, it was fun! I really wanted to tell my buddies about the awesome places we visited, but I couldn't. As far as they knew, I was in California becoming a star. *(Oh! Another secret about lies is that they don't last long…at all.)* While I was telling my friends all that 'stuff,' my parents were clueless about my dishonesty. I tried to hide it from them, making sure they didn't see the messages and always changing the subject when my mom saw a text that caught her off-guard, prompting her to ask me about it. It was only so long that I could hide in the dark before the light hit me.

We had come home for the holidays, and it was the Sunday before Christmas. I had just gotten out of church serving with the 2nd-graders and, while in the car, my mom told me a story…

One of my friend's moms came up to her after service and asked about how things were going with my acting. My mom was shocked and confused. Not one to lie, she set the record straight. Meanwhile, my friend (who was standing with her mom) was very upset and crushed to learn I had lied not only to her but everyone else. I felt horrible, knowing the whole time I should have done the right thing and told the truth from the beginning.

After getting a good, long lecture about **integrity** and **honesty**, coupled with me giving lots of apologies to my parents, I knew what I had to do.

I spent a good half-hour writing and rewriting a super long message, telling my friends everything: my lie, how sorry I was, and what I'd truly been doing while away. My fingers shook as I hit 'Send.' Knowing I probably lost all my friends didn't exactly make me feel good.

Later that day, I was in Target with my mom, and we were laughing about something when the phone started to buzz. Before she handed it to me, she read who it was. All she said was, *"They're texting you."* My heart **dropped**. I took a deep breath and opened the messages, bracing myself for a bunch of ***"I HATE YOU!"*** texts. As I began to read them, I was surprised! My friends didn't hate me! Were they ***disappointed***? Yes, but they were willing to forgive me and move on. My friends showed me a tremendous amount of grace, and I was very grateful for that.

When I returned to my Nana's house, I was still in shock—and a bit shook. I *still* couldn't wrap my mind around what just happened. My friends **FORGAVE** me! They actually ***FORGAVE*** me in like five minutes! *I sure wouldn't have forgiven me…*

I was still baffled when God brought to my remembrance how Jesus sacrificed His life and forgave us for way worse than what I had done. I wondered if God had let that whole situation go down the way it did to remind me how special and sacred Christ's sacrifice truly is. It sure changed the way I saw the entire situation with both Jesus and my friends!

Today, the relationship with my friends still isn't perfect. Some of them still haven't talked to me (the incident was very recent), not because they're mad necessarily, but more because they need some time to process it all—and I'm okay with that. I understand it takes some time to get over being deceived.

Another thing to keep in mind when you're trying to repair a relationship you might have broken is that it might take **time**. At the end of the day, you hurt them, and it's going to take **time** to get over it. Just give it to God and let Him do the rest.

Now, without me turning into your 'life coach,' I wrote my story and was vulnerable enough to not only share so that you might laugh and think I'm silly, but also to let you know you're not alone. We are all on this crazy joyride together called **"Being a Teen."** Although I might be new at it, trust me when I say: We all know what it's like to lose ourselves sometimes and do stupid stuff for approval. Let me be the first to let you know that God's got this! He knows you and all your silly, fun, and sometimes crazy plans. He loves you and approves of you in every way, so you can live your life knowing that your Heavenly Father loves you and that He's on this ride with you—every up and down, every slip and slide. Don't rush the process, because as soon as you get off this one, there's a whole new ride waiting for you with its own set of challenges. "Unfair!" you say?

Don't blame me! ***It's all a part of growing up!***

Supporting Cast Member
Elijah Hogan

Elijah Hogan is an aspiring Graphic Designer who hopes to start his own business after graduation in 2021. He currently does customized shoes for family and friends with different logos and characters. During his high school venture, he has played various sports and desires to attend college to pursue his career. With the support of his family and teachers, Elijah maintains the A/B Honor Roll. He attends church regularly and works to build a closer relationship with God. He resides in Dallas, Texas, with his grandparents and has two younger sisters he speaks to daily.

THE ACADEMIC STRUGGLE IS OVER!

Have you ever struggled with academics so much, you felt like giving up? Well, let me tell you how I once struggled with achieving passing grades and how I overcame it.

My struggles started when I was in elementary school. I had to complete homework and return the assignments the next day. Often, I didn't understand the questions and would get very frustrated behind my lack of understanding. My mom would try to help me by first showing me how to solve a problem. Then, she would tell me to do it…but I **couldn't**. Just that fast, I forgot how to do the work. So, I would just stare at the problem, hoping the answer would jump at me (or wait until she gave in and provided me with the answer). At the time, my mom didn't realize I had a problem with comprehension, so she made me sit there and do the work over and over until I got it right. I constantly cried because I couldn't come up with the correct answer.

My mom then asked our next-door neighbor to assist me with my homework. When

I went to my neighbor's house, he explained step-by-step what the question was asking me. Only then did I start to understand it a ***little*** better. Eventually, I got the point where I could solve the problems faster, which made me happy. I felt good about myself! I learned how to take my time with every question and not to give up.

Thinking back to when I lived with my mom, we moved around a lot, so I was never able to settle anywhere and get comfortable. My mom tried the best she could, but I had two sisters, which limited her time to really focus on me like that. When I moved in with my dad and grandparents, I was afforded more stability. Still, my academics suffered. When I brought home homework and asked my dad to help, we'd sit there for what felt like all day. He couldn't understand why I wasn't getting it, and he didn't have the patience to keep dealing with my lack of understanding.

My grandma reached out to other family members to help, which they did—but only when I was able to be taken to them. My dad couldn't consistently take me to the tutoring sessions due to his work schedule. My uncle was already in college at the time and, when he would come back to visit, he would help me from time to time. I believe the lack of consistency prevented me from learning the material at school as well as the other kids did, which caused me to be held back a year during that time. I didn't know the content well enough to be promoted to the next grade. My grandparents could only do so much because they were up in age, and the assignments from school weren't easy for them to understand either. My grandmother finally decided to reach out to other family members in hopes of finding a school that would be beneficial to my unique learning needs.

When I was in junior high school, things went well for me. It was good because, in every class, someone would help me with the homework and check over my work before I turned it in. My first class of the day was English, which I didn't really like. I knew, however, I had to do whatever it took to pass, which meant studying more before quizzes and tests. I would get nervous before any test and start to panic. When I calmed down a bit, I would concentrate and take my time by reading the question and breaking it down into parts so that I could fully understand what the question asked me. The

STAAR (**S**tate of **T**exas **A**ssessments of **A**cademic **R**eadiness) Test is still a struggle for me. I find myself having to retake it several times (even students who ***don't*** have a learning disability complain about the test and say it is nothing like the material that is taught in class).

While in junior high, I was officially diagnosed with a learning disorder called "Dyslexia." For those who may not know, dyslexia is a learning disorder that involves difficulty reading due to problems identifying speech sounds and learning how they relate to letters and words (aka *decoding*). It can also refer to having a disability that affects areas of the brain which process language and comprehension. Someone without that limitation can typically grasp concepts much quicker, whereas, for me, it takes a couple of times to find the solution.

Now that I'm in high school, I go to student support. They help students with their homework, tests, quizzes, and whatever else the student is having trouble with in class. In most instances, students aren't allowed to use their notes, but in my case, I am permitted to do so when I take quizzes and tests. Something else I have started doing is sitting in front of the class so I can focus, be involved, and not fall asleep. My meetings with student support began to help me a lot, and the teachers help me with gaining a better understanding of the work. I am grateful for their empathy concerning my situation. They go over my work step-by-step, check my answers, and evaluate my daily progress for every class.

After hard work and dedication, I was ready to take on a different type of school—one with a mission-focused learning environment. Their ***vision*** is dedicated to raising generations of well-rounded individuals who will realize their worth and purpose, find their interest and gifting, develop their skills, reach their highest potential, and meet the demands of this nation and world by receiving personalized educational experiences in a disciplined, nurturing, and character-building environment facilitated through partnerships between faculty, students, parents, and community. Their ***mission*** is to train and educate future generations of young men and women with wisdom, stature, and favor; to give students opportunities to become whole individuals, ready to serve the world by helping them reach their highest potential; and to provide in partnership with parents and community a well-rounded education within the context of American heritage. During orientation, the presenter had me blown away! I loved every minute of how focused they were to help **me** succeed!

The school is built much like a college campus, which preps students for changing between buildings rather than the typical hallways in high schools. The school was recommended by my cousin, who is an English teacher for Desoto ISD. The help and attention the teachers give me daily have elevated my confidence, understanding, and overall knowledge in my academics. My grades have improved these past two years dramatically by being at this school, and my family is so proud of the growth they see in me from day to day. The school also focuses on my future in college and career-related opportunities once I graduate in 2021.

My grandparents keep me in church and, by learning more and more about God and praying, it has helped me grow spiritually and assisted me with overcoming a lot of the depression and self-esteem issues that arose with having a condition like mine. My uncle inspires me as well because I witnessed him attend college, graduate with a degree, and return home to have a successful career. I figure if he can do it, so can I! He and his wife always tell me to keep up the good work when I show them my report card. They are so proud! I refuse to let them down.

I know God has a plan for me. I desire to go to college to study business and one day operate my own business doing something I'm passionate about and enjoy doing every day. I'm developing better study habits, so that won't be an issue at all when I attend college. I believe I am well-prepared for the journey. I've been told by several people, ***"It will be your mind that takes you where you want to be in life."***

As I reflect on the obstacles and heartaches I've endured throughout my childhood, I can honestly say I'm truly blessed and highly favored by God. With His help and guidance, I have pushed through the difficulties and continue to strive for academic greatness and athleticism. Baseball has become my favorite sport. It has brought many other opportunities to me, and I know if I don't continue to excel in academics, I will be unable to play (I make sure I stay on top of my schoolwork). I often sit in my room and read the Bible when I find myself feeling discouraged or defeated. I also love to draw and find it to be a way to relieve stress when I'm not feeling my best.

A lot of people may assume that because we are young, we don't encounter issues, get lonely, or fail to accomplish tasks. I believe age doesn't matter. I read all too often about teens who have committed suicide because the burdens they carry overtook their minds. School can be very stressful because not only are you trying to please your parents, but you want to make sure you pass to the next grade each year.

If I could sit down and talk with you face-to-face, I would tell you the only way to be successful is to first believe in yourself. Allow those who care about you the most to be your motivation. If you attend a school that does not offer student support for one-on-one teachings, don't be afraid to ask your teachers or counselors how to attend tutoring classes. You can even take the initiative to ask for practice work to take home. Speak up for yourself when you need to. Raise your hand. Ask your teachers to repeat something, especially if it doesn't make sense to you. From talking with my friends, I realized they had the same questions but felt like they would sound "dumb" if they asked to have something explained again. Teachers must learn there is not just one method of solving a problem. If you feel you have a different way that helps you understand it better, talk about it. You could be the source of relief that another student needs! If you have a support system and are willing to take on new challenges, you can't lose! However, the effort must start with you **wanting** to have patience and listen to what is being taught. If you start out thinking negatively, your outcome will not be successful.

I'm so happy to be a part of this opportunity to help someone else who may be struggling with the same issues as me. Hopefully, my story can help them see there's no need to give up. I had the choice of whether I would use my disability as an excuse not to be great and gain pity from others. With everything that has been instilled in me, it was up to me to take the knowledge I acquired and apply it to my everyday struggles.

I can do **ALL** this through **HIM** [Christ] who gives me strength! (Philippians 4:13)

Supporting Cast Member
Gracie Greene

Gracie Greene is an 18-year-old resident of Sienna Plantation, Texas. She attends Houston Community College. Some of her favorite hobbies include music (rap), writing, and styling hair. Gracie attends and volunteers her time at New Hope Church in Houston, where Pastor Carl Cherry is the Lead Student Pastor.

INSATIABLE

We **ALL** have something we want, crave, and desire…something that makes us insatiable. ***"Insatiable"*** means greedy or having an unfulfilled desire for something. It doesn't matter who you are or what gender or race you identify with; we are all insatiable people and won't stop until we get that "thing" we believe is of the utmost importance. **For WHAT**? The reasons are vast, to include:

- *"I'll look nice in that!"*
- *"It's trending right now. I must have it!"*
- *"I'm addicted. I can't live without it!"* (That not only refers to alcohol and drugs; it can also be materialistic things like money, clothes, and jewelry.)

You may be wondering, *"So, Gracie, what was that "thing" that made* **you** *be labeled as insatiable?"* Good question! I'm glad you asked!

For me, it was popularity. Yes, **popularity**. Growing up, I wanted so badly to be popular and did any and everything I could to achieve that status. I even let people walk all over me, mistreat me, and make fun of me. I didn't care, as long as

I was **popular**. At one point, I even considered selling my soul just to be accepted within the popular clique *(thank **GOD**, I am over **THAT** phase)*!

Still, some young and grown people are caught up in the grips of being popular, to the point they are allowing the desire to take over their lives. Let me say this right now: **STOP IT!** If you were meant to be "popular," it will happen without you even trying! That was a lesson I had to learn the hard way.

Let me tell you what happened…

It started way back in second grade, which, by the way, was the year I met my "popular" best friend. We didn't start out as friends, though. She was rude to me in school, but outside of school, she was nice. It was like that every day. But, since she wanted to be friends outside of school, I used to hang out with her because I knew she was "cool" *(she and I are no longer friends because she doesn't know* **how** *to be a friend).*

I refused to tell my mom about the mean way she treated me because that would have been unpopular. I chose to hang around her and some of her friends, even though I do remember one other girl treating me just as poorly as "my friend." I hated how they treated me, but popularity had its stronghold on me.

As I got older, it didn't get any better. I always ended up associating with two-faced people. I'm not proud to admit I used to do the same thing to other girls and boys: be nice one minute and rude the next. I did whatever I had to do to be accepted. I'm ashamed to say, at one point, I **LIKED** hurting other people's feelings. It is said, *"Hurt people HURT PEOPLE,"* and I was hurting deeply. All that changed when one day, the "fake friend" became a "real friend." She was actually kind to me **ALL** day in school (I think it was because she moved to another neighborhood and didn't have any other kids to play with.)

Now, *before* that day of kindness, I had stopped hanging out with her because my mom found out about how mean she was to me. Then, when **her** mom heard about it, she made "my friend" apologize. (I thought she was kidding around at first. I waited all day for an eye roll or **something** during class, but nothing happened.) Not only was she nice, but her friends were, too.

There's an adage that says, *"You can catch more flies with honey than you can with vinegar."*

Another says, *"Kill them with kindness."* **Both** mean that when you're kind to a person, it just may overpower their ignorance and rudeness. That's been my experience. Many times, when I am kind to someone who has been rude to me, they start behaving differently by being kinder to me. Now, I'm not saying ***everyone*** makes that change. Some people are cold-hearted and couldn't care less about others' feelings. If that is the case, you should accept it and move on. Admittedly, it took me a while to "get it."

Growing up, I tended to gravitate to people who were "cool," not the ones who were more like me. As a result, my friendships rarely lasted for long periods. Those who didn't want me in their circle, no matter how hard I tried, proved to be toxic. Soon, sadness and loneliness became my best friends.

For a while, I was homeschooled. During that time, I had moments when I would reflect on how I treated other students. I was remorseful and had plenty of time to think about my past and how I got myself into that position in the first place. I had no one to blame but myself…but the remorse didn't last long!

When I returned to public school in the seventh grade, "popularity" came back with me in full force—along with the mistreatment. Some boys teased me, calling me "fat" and "ugly." They also made fun of my religion and would constantly drum up arguments just to cause drama. On top of it all, I was also dealing with some rude girls in my neighborhood who I considered friends at one point. ***What kind of "friend" teases you, gossips about you, and tells lies on you to not only your peers but also their mothers?!*** Eventually, I got to the point where I couldn't take the verbal abuse anymore. When my self-esteem was at its lowest, I **snapped**!

After I graduated high school, I was tired, sad, and angry at the same time. I just wanted **real** friends, so I decided to cut off all the toxic people in my life. It was easier than I thought! I simply stopped hanging around those people and let God lead the way. It wasn't an overnight process, though. It took a while to break free from popularity's stronghold on my life.

Once I was free from the toxicity of fake friendships, I found myself rushing into others *(I suppose that's why many ended as quickly as they began)*. I was desperately seeking someone I could talk to. I used to meet someone new, wait a while to exchange telephone numbers, and, after texting and talking for a few days, if nothing "magical" happened (in terms of a friendship blossoming), I quickly ended **all** my efforts. I had to make the conscious choice to stop forcing friendships.

NOTE: You cannot make people like you.

Ever since I stopped trying to force my friendship on others, I made much better friends with those **God** placed in my life. I appreciate them now more than I would have in the past. The amazing people I've met not only came from Tosha Dearbone's "Positive Express" *(a local youth group for young ladies that focuses on self-esteem and other issues in society)*, but also from the church as well! I volunteer at the church on the weekends and let me tell you: Those I have met are so loving and genuinely kind. We hang out upstairs at church and talk about God, relationships, food, what's trending in Hollywood…whatever pops into our minds. We also eat so much food until it feels like our stomachs are going to pop! The more I get to know each of them, the more grateful I am that I removed those negative influences from my life. I am no longer as stressed out as I once was, and I've learned from my mistakes.

If your situation is **anything** like mine *was*, I encourage you to stop hanging out with toxic people. Stop letting "things" or people run your life. I promise: You will feel **SO** much better! After all, being insatiable is spiritually, mentally, ***AND*** physically draining!

If you are someone who wants nothing more than the "popularity stamp"…if you're so desperate to be "cool"…stop investing your time into trying to *MAKE* it happen. Make friends with people who will appreciate and care about who you are becoming. Allow God to set you on the path for which you are destined. He will make it come to pass—***if you believe.*** I know what I'm talking about. That's what happened to me!

Being **INSATIABLE** will only bring you heartache, anger, pain, stress, and unnecessary suffering. Please step back and let God take control. Your life will be **MUCH** easier when you do!

Supporting Cast Member John Oakes

John Oakes is a 14-year-old freshman in high school. His favorite subjects are Mathematics and Physical Education. He is an Illinois native who aspires to be a Dentist and Barbershop Owner. John has an interest in Martial Arts and previously studied Tae Kwon Do. He's an ultimate fan of entertainment wrestling and enjoys bowling. John believes you achieve success by being productive and always arriving on time to every commitment.

THE DIFFICULT AND AWESOME LIFE OF A TEENAGER

For some reason, a lot of grownups think kids don't go through *anything*. It may be hard for them to think back to the days of their youth, but if they would, they will likely recall the challenges **they** faced and realize being a teenager is not always easy.

I hope my chapter is not boring to you because my life is far from it. Well, thinking about that previous statement…I sometimes *feel* it is boring. I don't like sitting in the house doing nothing. I'm sure you feel the same way at times. If you are interested in knowing what I have to say, I imagine you will have fun reading this! In school, we are tasked with reading all the time. When you can choose what to read, make sure you pick a book you believe you will like. I hope this book becomes one of your favorite reads!

I am 14 years old. I am looking forward to becoming an adult, but it seems to be taking **SO** long…*too long, if you ask me.* Every year, I look forward to my birthday. Those days are great to celebrate, as it helps me realize I am one year closer to adulthood. However, I will always remember how this time felt in my life. Are my days good? Are they bad? Recently, my answer has been **both**. I see the good and the bad in each day. During these teenage years, I am learning and want to share with you what I think.

Every day, I wake up and plan to do my best. A lot of teenagers don't like school, but I like going to class. I eat breakfast every single morning and enjoy going to different restaurants on the weekends. I then grab my book bag, put it on my back, and focus on the day ahead. I always try to leave the house early because I like going out and breathing in the fresh air. I don't like it when the bus comes late, especially when the weather is bad. I also don't like the days when class starts late. Sometimes, the teachers are in a meeting when most of us first get to class. The late start makes the day shorter, significantly reducing the time we have to complete our assignments. *(I am not a fan of days that feel longer than usual.)*

At night, I sometimes sit and look up at the moon. Night after night, I watch and see how a different version of it is revealed. I don't stay up too late, but watching the night sky calms me. I have so many thoughts that come to mind as I reflect on my day. Everything around me is so quiet. The city seems to slow down, affording me the time just to relax. I don't want to bounce around all the time, so relaxing is what I do to close out the day as I prepare my mind for the next school day.

I am glad to be in high school now. Not long ago, I remember wondering how high school life would be. I recall being nervous, thinking about how gigantic the school would be and wondering how well I would do. At the time, I wasn't sure how many of my old classmates would join me on my new venture into academia. The first couple of weeks of high school turned out just fine. As I looked around, I saw so many students I knew from my old grammar schools. *(When you move forward into something new, you still want to see something familiar such as people and things you recognize.)* It made me more comfortable seeing some of the students I knew. When I walk the hallways, those who know me call me "Gucci John." I really like that name. I've always liked it when people care enough to give you a nickname. I have had a lot of nicknames over the years, but you can just call me "John."

One thing I didn't expect with the change in atmosphere was for some of those same people I used to associate with begin to react differently towards me. Most are okay, but some don't act the same. Some of the same students I once talked to or thought were my friends may not speak to me at times—if at all. I suppose it's a part of teenage life. I was forewarned that kids may not be as friendly, or their personality may change at this age as they figure out their identity. While they are searching for who they are and what they want to be in life, I just want good friends.

I believe that anywhere there is good, bad can be present. I am not trying to be negative; that is just the way I see it. One thing I dislike is hearing about bullies and teens fighting. ***How can people treat each other like that?*** I never would. People were not made to be the same. There will always be kids who act differently than you. If teenagers don't learn how to get along, even when they disagree, they will continue that toxic behavior into their adult lives. Teens should help one another and treat each other right. Someone could be struggling with school or having problems at home, and you would never know.

Don't be a terrible person; choose to be a positive force in others' lives.

I don't like it when teenagers drink and smoke. Our bodies are continually changing and growing. We should take care of our bodies. Even in Biology class, we learned certain things are outright unhealthy. Personally, I drink a lot of water to help maintain good health. I see the changes my body is going through when I look in the mirror. I am getting taller and hope to one day be over six feet tall. Puberty is changing my voice and has now given me acne, which I despise. When I see that, I know it is a challenge of mine and something many other teenagers go through. Still, I can't help but wish it was not a part of growing up. All of us teens will experience bodily changes. It's a big deal, so you want to take care of yourself!

When I turn on the television to watch the news, it seems as if they hardly ever report a lot of good things. Most often, they talk about the bad things that happened that day. Every day, the reporters mention someone getting killed. Much of the time, it is due to gun violence. Guns seem to be **everywhere**! Too many people are willing to kill others for no good reason. I get so tired of hearing that type of news every day. If you can walk away or call the police, do it! Sadly, a lot of the news stories talk about people around my age. No one wants to die young. As for me, I want to live until I'm at least 100 years old…or even 200, if that is somehow possible. Our lives shouldn't end because **someone else** decides to take it away.

Two years ago, I went to Washington, D.C., for the "March for Our Lives Rally." We protested violence and shootings that have happened in certain schools and communities. There were a lot of people watching us march. We walked and walked…and walked. There were students **everywhere** I looked, carrying the signs they made. Today, when I look around, it seems as if nothing has changed. As a matter of fact, during this school year, one of the students at my school was killed. The principal had grief counselors come to our school, just in case any of the students needed to talk about how they felt. I do not have the specifics about how the student was murdered, but I have heard some of the details. I want nothing more than for the killing of our youth to stop, but it just keeps happening.

I want this time in my life to pass by fast. I still plan to work hard in school because I want to keep getting good grades. School is my priority. I often think about seeing more than the neighborhoods similar to the one where I live. I like my community, but there are so many places I have yet to go. I want to travel and visit more states here in the U.S., especially Ohio. I really want to go there to visit the Cedar Point Amusement Park. When I travel with my family, I like going to different hotels, especially the big ones that have a lot of space. I always hope there is a waterpark on the premises or at least a beach nearby.

I am excited about driving at sixteen. I already looked up the total hours of driving needed after I receive my driver's permit in order to obtain my license. My school district is changing, and I am concerned about Driver's Ed now. I really want to take the course during my sophomore year. I no longer have a favorite car, so I am willing to buy just about any vehicle. At the age of 17, I will graduate from high school. I can't even say which one, since the final decision regarding the school district's reconfiguration plan has not been finalized yet.

After my 18th birthday, I will prepare to go to college. I thought I had time to decide which college I want to attend. I am being told I should think about that ***now***. I do not know what school I want to go to yet. That is a big decision! I will take my time and decide when I am ready. I know I often want to rush time because I'm ready for certain things to happen. I'll take my time, though, and experience life. I have a lot to accomplish!

At this point, I cannot say all of what my life will entail, but I do know what I am planning to become. I don't want my life to be unhappy constantly. Even with being a happy person, I sometimes get mad or frustrated when things don't happen the way I feel they should. I can't and won't give up, though! When I was younger, I learned just to breathe my way through obstacles and keep going. I want **you** to focus on being *happy*. No matter what happens in life, do not quit!

I know I don't have the answer to everything, but saying *"I don't know"* is not acceptable to me. I want to learn and study different things. If I don't understand something, I ask questions and research things I see are new or confusing. Daily, I use Google on my phone to search until I find what I desire. I recommend you use anything you can to gather the information that can help you solve problems, become better, and mature. Even if you must look up things or talk to a teacher, do what you must to get what you need.

I keep hearing people say that ***we*** are the future. They want to believe in today's youth. We have a lot of things we must deal with, but we have the power to change the world for the better. With all the teenagers I see receiving awards and meeting celebrities, we are doing awesome! We can use whatever platform we are given to do great things. I believe we all want a chance to be in charge. I know we all want our lives to be successful. Let's not mess things up for those coming after us. We are smart! **This world needs what we have to give!**

Supporting Cast Member La'Tajia Thompson

La'Tajia Thompson is a 14-year-old Houston, Texas native. She is an 8th-grader at Lake Olympia Middle School who aspires to graduate from Hightower High school and attend college to earn a degree in Criminal Justice as a Criminal Lawyer. With her career choice, La'Tajia's passion is to help others prove their innocence and stand up for what is right.

WALKING IN MY OWN SHADOW

It all started for me in elementary school. I was seven years old, in the 2nd grade, and kind of shy. I was also mature in areas that other kids were not. It seemed as if **suddenly**, everything changed.

I recall walking to recess when a little boy walked up to me, called me "fat," and took off running and laughing. I ignored him. Then, the following day, he did it again. I felt uncomfortable and did not know who to tell, so I just stayed silent and let him continue to torment me for about two more months. When I got tired of his constant bullying, instead of telling an adult, I began to act out in class. On time, I climbed under the desk, flipped it over, and ran out of the classroom.

When my teacher asked me questions, and I didn't respond, she sent me to the principal's office. I refused to talk about my problem even then, so they called my mother. She spoke to me over the phone and told me to sit down and stop clowning around in school. Even **she** did not know what was going on with me because I didn't tell ***ANYONE*** about what was happening. That call only served to make me angrier. I returned to class, and the tormenting started all over again.

One day, I was sent to the counselor's office because they were concerned I would harm someone else or myself. It was in that space when I began to tell what was going on. The counselor listened—**and then tried to make me feel as if I was the one in the wrong!** Basically, she ignored my cries for help and threatened me with action against my "bad behavior" if I did not stop acting up in class.

Days went by, and the name-calling kept going. That continued until I was in the 5th grade when yet **another** boy decided he would bully me. The day came when he called me out of my name. By that time, my anger had built up and took over. I stabbed him with a pencil and did not stop until I saw blood. The teacher screamed and told me to go to the office. I was then suspended for three days. My mom was so upset. She kept asking me, *"Why didn't the teacher or principal* *do anything about the little boy?"* I just kept saying, *"I don't know."*

After my suspension was over, I returned to school, where all the kids began saying things like, *"She is **crazy**! I wouldn't want to mess with her!"*

Then, on another occasion, I was sitting at my desk and asked the teacher for an eraser. Instead of her handing it to me, she decided to throw it! I immediately reacted by shoving the desk at her. She shouted, ***"GET OUT OF THE CLASS! GO TO THE OFFICE!"*** So, I grabbed all my stuff and walked toward the front exit door. The school officer and other teachers grabbed me and tried to tell me to come back. I was so mad and didn't want to hear anything they had to say. They rushed and called my mom, who seemed to appear in a matter of *seconds*.

An impromptu meeting was held with her, and she was very upset about how they were handling things. When she asked me why my behavior was becoming out of control, I explained this boy was bullying me and that no one was doing anything to stop it. My mom then directed her questioning at the principal and staff:

Why is no one listening to my child?

Why do you insist my daughter isn't telling the truth about being called names?

What about the teacher who threw an eraser at her?

WHY WAS NOTHING BEING DONE ABOUT THESE SITUATIONS?!

Instead of properly handling the situations in school on their own, they chose to call my mom about my "bad behavior" **every** time. A meeting with the counselor was scheduled, and the principal assured us a follow-up would be done with all involved.

After about a week, both of my parents came to the school for the meeting. The principal spoke with the bully and learned I was being honest about what he had been doing to me. However, they could not tell my parents exactly what was done about his actions. What they did say was, *"He will no longer be messing with her."*

Not long after the incident, the teacher resigned from the school. I am left to believe that if my parents had never gotten involved, the bullying would have continued unpunished.

Not long after the incidents were resolved, my mom scheduled me for a visit with a therapist. When I walked into her office for the first time, I was surprised to see someone who resembled me. She was tall (maybe six feet), African American, and kind of stocky. She introduced herself, and I did the same. She asked questions about my home, school, and then me. I remember telling her I was being picked on for being tall. She shared with me that people did the same thing to her until she started playing basketball. She stated she had to start embracing her height and that I would have to do the same. Those words made me feel a little better because I actually saw someone sitting before me who was not only okay with her height but also had an excellent career.

I took her advice and started shifting my focus. When I was teased about my stature, I would say, ***"I love my height!"*** I guess it's safe to say the therapist helped me with my self-confidence. My mom continued to help me as well by showing me the tallest man in the Bible, Goliath (it also says that Adam and Eve were 15 feet tall, but I'm not sure if that is a myth). Nonetheless, that knowledge gave me more confidence to walk with my head held high!

As I transitioned to middle school, things seemed to be going well for a while—until the day my teacher and I had words, and she had to call my mother. I recall her telling my mom that she was terrified of me due to my height and size. *How funny is it that a teacher thought that because I was tall, I was also strong? LOL!* Never have I tried to fight anyone or be a bully. Now, don't get me wrong: I was not going to sit idly by and allow someone to hit me either. Anyway, whatever she and my mom discussed had stopped the teacher from messing with me ever again.

While in the 6th grade, I was diagnosed with borderline diabetes. I wasn't put on any medications at that time, but the doctors wanted me to watch what I ate, exercise more, and consume lots of water. Those tasks were not easy for me, mainly because I was a picky eater. As a result, my mom didn't force me too much to do what was right. After a year, I went to see my doctor again and was told, *"You are diabetic."* Instantly, I began to have flashbacks about my grandmother. The same year I was diagnosed with complications associated with diabetes and breathing issues, my grandmother passed away. I do, however, remember watching as she pricked herself with needles and had to take insulin shots every day. All I could think was, *"I need to get my stuff together!"*

I started taking a diabetic medication called Metformin and tried to do what was right for my health by eating better and walking more. For a while, things were going well. Then, the day came when they gave me a testing meter. *"Lord, why me? Why do I have to stick myself not once, but twice daily? Why must I take these two horse pills?!"* I hated taking them…and still do. Moving forward, I began taking my medicine regularly and started to notice a drop in my weight. That gave me even **more** of a confidence boost! I was confident enough to know I could accomplish ***ANYTHING*** I put my mind to.

Another crucial lesson in my growth came when one day, my gym teacher noticed I wasn't dressing out for class. She told me that dressing was half the grade, with the rest being participation in the activities. I wasn't trying to hear it. I didn't want to dress out because I refused to change clothes in front of others (yes, I felt less confident about my size again). I concerned myself with that others would say about me. Guess what the teacher did? You guessed correctly if you said, *"She called your mom."* I hated the fact that she made that call because I **knew** my mom would be angry about me not following directions. Although she was upset, she encouraged me with the following words:

"In order for others to notice your confidence, you must first have confidence in yourself!"

I allowed those words to settle into my spirit and promised to do better. When I returned to school and dressed out for class, I walked with confidence because I loved **ME!**

I leave **YOU** with these words of encouragement:

Know who you are and **WHO'S** you are – ***GOD'S daughter or son!***

Supporting Cast Member Shakeyra Williams

Shakeyra Williams is an aspiring Artist who hopes to major in Animation after graduation in 2021. She is a member of her high school's Student Council and National Art Society Club. She also likes to travel with her family. With continuous motivation from her mom, she is looking forward to graduating from high school and starting her own business. She is learning that depending on God is what she needs to succeed, and consults Him in her decision making. Shakeyra currently resides in Lewisville, Texas, with her mom, stepdad, and two sisters, with a little brother expected in May 2020.

MOTIVATION WAS THE KEY TO MY ACADEMIC SUCCESS

The academic struggle is a common thing for many teens. I would know; I'm one of them. I never liked going to school because I was unable to learn as quickly as others, leaving me to think I was dumb or just lazy. Sometimes, I would even say, *"This is too hard!"* or *"I'm not doing it!"*—all because I failed to understand most of the work. Many of my teachers had to show me on paper, which sometimes helped me understand what everyone else already understood. I was even a slow test-taker. My teachers would often instruct me to either come earlier in the morning or stay after school for tutoring *(I disliked doing the latter because I was ready to go **home**).*

I hated school with a passion! I knew people talked about me when I didn't understand a problem or question (not that I cared). Math was always my problem subject. I rarely understood it right away, so I would give up and not care about the work. My train of thought every time was, *"Why do the work if I don't understand it?"* My mom did her best to assure me I wasn't as "dumb" as I felt when she said, *"Every teacher teaches differently. Maybe one-on-one tutoring would help."*

Everyone says the elementary years are the easiest. That's not true for someone like me who had trouble with comprehension. As a little girl, I never understood what it really meant to be on the honor roll or be the highest achiever in class. It all started to make sense to me when we would have our annual awards day, and I would see other students being called for different academic accomplishments. Somehow, my name wasn't among the list of achievers. I figured it wasn't a big deal, as long as I passed to the next grade, right? **How important was *elementary* anyway?** Those were my thoughts until I realized the most challenging test of the year would answer those questions.

It wasn't long before I was introduced to the **S**tate of **T**exas **A**ssessments of **A**cademic **R**eadiness (STAAR) Test. For the first time, I wasn't the only one threatened with being held back if I didn't meet the minimum standard score. I remember saying to myself, *"What is the point of this test? **Can't they see I struggle enough?**"* Once the results came, my mom would sit down with me and try to determine what parts I had the most trouble with. We would then attend a meeting with the principal and my teachers to discuss if they believed I was ready to move on to the next grade. **Just how successful would I be, especially when I didn't know the *previous* year's material?**

By the time I hit middle school, Math looked like a foreign language to me. I still didn't put much effort into it because I thought asking for help would get me going. That idea failed to work. I simply did what I had always done: forgot how to do the work after the teacher took the time to show me. I just wanted Math to be over for good! During the 7th and 8th grades, it still didn't get any better. I hardly ever passed any Math test, and when I did, it was after a retest with additional help. During this time in my educational venture, I was also tested for learning disabilities, but none were recognized.

Due to my heightened frustration, I became rebellious at home and blamed others for my struggles. There were times when my mom asked about in-class assignments and homework, and I'd just say, *"I didn't receive any from the teacher."* Well, my mom was too smart to accept

that excuse! With the way the school's communication with parents is set up, she received phone calls, texts, and emails about my grades, absences, etc. That didn't stop me from lying, though. I would explain away the lack of work in the following ways:

"I don't know where the assignments are."

OR

"I've completed it already. I'm waiting for the teacher to grade it."

Weeks would go by with no grade produced, and I was back at the start of answering to my mom why the grade remained a **ZERO**. She then began to email ***ALL*** my teachers consistently regarding my progress in class. They also made plans for me to stay after school for tutoring or make-up work.

That started in middle school and continued up until my sophomore year. Today, I have taken on the responsibility to communicate with my teachers to ask for the help I need.

Once I reached high school, I remember the day when I walked into my 9th-grade Geometry class and was handed a test I had completely forgotten about and didn't complete the required review. I received a grade of 34 out of a possible 100. By making a habit of not being prepared, I spent the rest of that year working to bring up my grade. It was incredibly difficult!

Over time, I began to get better at Math because people noticed I needed help and decided to tutor me. I also started taking online classes (once we found out it was an option), which helped me tremendously because I was at home and had better access to ask my family for help. The teachers were also very understanding and would meet with me to help with any questions I had. As a result, my grades got better. Back in middle school, I would be failing every class and barely passing by the end of the year; in high school, I was passing with not just Cs, but Bs!

Every once in a while, I still tend to get a little lazy, which results in procrastination and puts me behind in class. My teachers would then call or send emails to my mom that said:

"Lazy. Unmotivated. Not living up to her potential. Daydreams. Needs to work harder. Doesn't try her best. Doesn't pay attention. Needs to focus. If she would just apply herself, her grades will increase."

When my mom would approach me with the teachers' feedback, I would say, *"I don't know what they are talking about"*—but I did because, again, it went back to me not understanding the work.

I'm grateful for the people who took the time to help me. I'm no longer as stressed as I used to be. Even though I struggled in the majority of my classes, eventually, I got better because I decided to pick up the slack. I now have more confidence in my abilities. Another thing I did to overcome my academic struggles was asked my mom to teach me outside of school, which led to the online classes. I began looking at example problems carefully and taking my own notes to help me understand how the answer was found. YouTube is also another resource I use at home when I'm unsure. There are tons of sites that have practice problems. My counselors assumed since I had a hard time staying focused in class, online classes wouldn't be a good fit for me. Ever since I started the courses online, I have truly done so much better. It was even better when my mom helped me. To this day, she continues to assist me with my work with no questions asked. I am very thankful to have a mother like her. Without her, I know I wouldn't understand the work as much as I do now.

I always wanted to impress my mom and stepdad by being the best I could be, although I was never strong enough to take honors classes or be as fast of a learner as my younger sister. Still, I never stop trying to better my mindset to achieve higher grades. I often think about how difficult college may be for me and think, *"Do I have to repeat the same struggles, or does it get easier?"* My new study habits have taught me to focus and keep applying the study skills that will continue to benefit me in my last year of high school and college.

I had to find out for myself if my issue was with the lack of understanding of the work or the way it was presented to me. It seems every teacher has a different technique for working out problems. I became frustrated with them and myself. I know my mom disliked when I had the ***"I can't do it"*** attitude. She kept encouraging me until I had the **motivation** to try. Once I tried and succeeded, I was very pleased. My mom takes the time to teach me how to solve problems or questions in ways I can understand. Not only is that helpful, but it has also taught me the importance of mothers in our lives. Most of us could not make it in life without them. For some, the opposite is true: fathers fill that role, and that's understandable.

Most recently, I have been able to take Math, History, and English online at home. We have concluded that one-on-one studying was more beneficial for me. For those thinking that because the work is home-based, it's super easy – you would be wrong. Online students put in just as much time, if not **more**. There are tons of homework assignments and quizzes to complete, along with midterms, tests, and finals on the school campus. I no longer doubt whether I will pass or not because I am well-prepared. We are waiting for the day when I finally walk across the stage to receive my diploma. It will be an amazing day, primarily because my mom is the main one who has helped me get to where I am. Along the way, there were a few teachers I liked, only because they did what was expected of them and went above and beyond to ensure I was successful in their classes.

I have watched myself grow mentally, emotionally, and spiritually. I often look for scriptures to encourage me when I am having "a moment." Following is one that I like *(my parents are always there to break it down when I don't fully understand)*:

"Let us not become weary in doing good, for at the proper time we will reap a harvest if we do not give up" **(Galatians 6:9).**

In other words, don't let whatever is bothering you drain you of your energy. Instead, keep pushing and watch how it will benefit you in the long run…**if you show endurance.** Thus far, that has been a great life lesson!

My advice to you is to **always** ask for help, no matter how little the situation is. The support you receive will suffice in the end and likely be worth it. Never be embarrassed to ask someone to help you with something you don't understand, and don't let anyone make you feel dumb or like a nuisance for needing that help.

LET MY STORY BE YOUR MOTIVATION!

I want to leave you with ten tips to go by that helped me conquer my fears and challenges when I faced academic difficulties:

1. Be engaged, take notes, and listen.
2. Keep up to date with your homework.
3. Have an organizational system in place.
4. Establish a routine.
5. Have daily and weekly objectives in place.
6. Do not procrastinate.
7. Unplug, log off, mute, and power down.
8. Manage your stress.
9. Get tested for any learning disabilities.
10. Take advantage of all the technology available.

I hope my story is an eye-opener for someone else who may be feeling like dropping out of school or contemplating ending their life due to the pressure of being like others. I encourage you to be yourself and find what works best for you.

Supporting Cast Member Shatoria Stanford

Shatoria Stanford is 16 years old and loves to sing. She sometimes writes her own songs and using singing as a coping mechanism. She admits that Math and self-love are areas she struggles with. She is now receiving the help and support she needs in both areas since relocating from Texas to Louisiana. She states, *"If I could describe my life in one word, it would be **'ROLLERCOASTER.'** However, my struggles and all the pain I endured have made me the person I am today."*

UNFAVORABLE DECISIONS

"You don't know what you have until it is gone."

Right now, that quote sums up my 16-year-old life. Although I have a good head on my shoulders, I sometimes feel that is not the case. In life, we all have the power of choice. Often, those choices are made based on temporary feelings. Recently, I did a little bit of experimenting and made some choices that most would consider unwise. Those ***unfavorable decisions*** were made during the latter part of my freshman year in high school.

High school's "environment" can treat you both good and bad at the same time. For a while, I felt alienated and separated from many people. That wasn't necessarily a new feeling for me because I am usually a quiet person—sociable at times, but mostly, I keep to myself. Overall, my freshman year was good and seemed to fly by really fast.

And so, my story begins…

I am not happy about the decision I made to lose my virginity at the age of fourteen. With the pressures of wanting to fit in with my peers, I found myself wanting to be somebody I wasn't. Somewhere along the way, I lost sight of my authentic self. I have also smoked weed and drank liquor before. During the time I made those reckless decisions, I was living with my daddy, aunt, and grandmother in Houston, Texas, while my mama lived in Louisiana with my other siblings. I know I disappointed my mama in the process. I am young and didn't live up to her expectations. My mama wants the best for all her children and always tells us how much she loves us. Out of all my mama's kids, I'm the one who's probably experienced the most pain. I struggle a lot with low self-esteem and am also very sensitive, taking **everything** to heart.

The reason I was separated from my mama and siblings was that she dated a man who molested me while she was gone. That day, my mama had left my older sisters in charge of watching me, along with my grandfather. I thank God my sister was in the room with me because when she woke up, he left the room. When my mama picked up my sister and me from the bus stop the following day, I immediately told her. She quickly called him on the phone to confront him. While he did admit to coming into my room, he denied touching me. My mama called the police and did everything else possible to protect me, including kicking him out of the house. When **C**hild **P**rotective **S**ervices (CPS) came to the school to question my siblings and me, I was fearful of what would happen. I knew that despite what happened to me, my mama loved that man and already had a baby with him.

Before that incident, my mama always told us that **nobody** had the right to touch us inappropriately and if it did happen—*even if it was a family member*—she wanted to know. As a result, when the molestation was brought to light, I had to go through many interviews with detectives, CPS, and hospital staff—so many to the point that my mama got very upset. She wanted to know what was taking them so long to address the situation.

Next thing we knew, my mom's boyfriend relocated to Dallas, Texas, with an ex-girlfriend. He also spread rumors **(LIES!)** about me, saying that my mama *made* me say he touched me because he didn't want to be with her anymore. **That enraged me!** Thank God for the text messages he sent to my mother in the weeks prior, ***begging her*** not to leave him *(she wanted to* *end the relationship because he didn't want to make changes to his lifestyle).*

I remember overhearing my mama talking to his family members on the phone, and they told her that he had been doing those kinds of things and getting away with it. No one ever came forward because they knew his mom was ill and didn't want to cause her any worry. That made my mama mad because she had dated that man on and off for 12 years before even *considering* allowing him to move in with us. She kept saying, ***"If his family knew about those things, they should have told me!"*** They knew she had children in the home, with five of them being **GIRLS**! Eventually, one of his family members agreed to write a statement because he tried to molest her daughter as well. I truly felt bad for my mama and all she went through, as some believed what happened…and some didn't.

I then started having issues in school. When teachers would talk about things like rape or molestation in class, I would run out the door. I spoke with a counselor from time to time but did not feel she was really helping me. I fell into a state of depression and became suicidal. I started to cut on myself and write out ways to commit suicide. After I started having issues in school, and my mama learned just how **tragic** the effects were, she moved me to Louisiana with her. She felt I needed to be closer to her so that she could help me and get the help I needed outside of our home.

I recall having nightmares when it felt like someone was smothering me. I would yell for my mama, but she could never hear me. Meanwhile, the voices in my head told me to kill myself. Thankfully, my mama had me to start sleeping with her so that she could pray over and watch me. I even remember her taking me to her pastor so he could pray over me, too.

My mama continued trying to pursue pressing charges against the man who touched me. We even rode back and forth between Louisiana and Texas for more interviews. When my mama got tired of running back and forth with **no** progress being made in the case *(two years had passed)*, she told them we were done. Shortly after, a detective contacted her stating there was nothing more that could be done because a judge and jury would have a hard time trying to convince the District Attorney I was molested. He said it was possible I was sleeping and just

thought that man was trying to touch me, making the accusation a "mistake."

I was left to feel hurt and disappointed. Although others thought I was lying, my mama told me she believed me and would **never** doubt what I said nor how I felt. Every day that passed, I could tell the situation was bothering her. I thought, *"Maybe I should've just kept everything to myself."* That wouldn't have been a possibility, even if I **did** choose to keep silent because my younger sister was in bed with me at the time – and she tells **everything**, even to this day.

One day, I heard my mama telling someone that she had to forgive my molester, as that is what God told her to do. She went on to explain that one thing about a child molester is that they often try again. As for the man who touched me, she said the next time, he may not be so lucky; one day, he **will** get jail time for all the other times he *thought* he got away with it.

My mama is a very strong woman. I know sometimes, it takes a lot to try to be there for ten children, but she does it! There were times I've seen her cry, but most often, I see her praising God. I know she's been through a lot and continues to want the best for her children, which is why I try my best to do well in school.

When I was 12 years old, I thought about committing suicide because I felt like I wasn't good enough for anyone or anything. I believed the only way to stop the pain and torment I felt was to try and take my life. Most people didn't take me seriously and thought I was attention-seeking. With them saying that, it only made me feel **worse** about myself. As a result, I choose not to open up to people about my problems. I don't talk to anyone, including my mama, about my issues because I fear being judged. Unfortunately, holding everything in slowly turns into depression that causes anxiety and triggers other negative emotions.

I smile a lot while holding my real feelings inside. I don't want people to ask me if I'm okay or inquire about what's wrong because I wouldn't give them a straightforward answer. Even though I'm a teenager, I'm not one who requires having a lot of friends. Unlike those who think so, I do not want the attention they believe I seek. Slowly, I am reverting to my old self…*which isn't the best thing to do.* I overthink a lot and reflect on my past, which causes me to cry myself to sleep at times. Believe me: I want to do better. I don't want to lie in the confines of my room on my phone all day.

I have been bullied a lot in school about my weight. People have written horrible things about me in the bathroom on the walls. Bullying was another reason I once contemplated suicide. My mama has put me in counseling, although at one point, my mental health was so bad, I had to be put in a hospital for 14 days *(I don't think my stay there helped much)*. Although my mama supports me, I still feel depressed a lot and can't seem to get a foothold on where to start picking up the pieces of my life. I want and receive help, but for some reason, I just don't feel like I'm getting any better at times.

Music has always been my coping mechanism. I enjoy listening to all types of music. I sometimes write my own songs when I have time or when I am not feeling like myself. I can't go a day without music. It brings out another side of me through both my highs and lows. I have a passion for singing, although I don't do it often *(I get the gift of singing from my daddy's side of the family)*. Most often, I sing to myself because I am shy. I dream of being the CEO of my own business one day…which requires me getting and doing better. I want people to know who Shatoria is through the legacy I leave with those who will come after me *(my younger siblings can't look up to me if I continue to stay in my room being depressed)*.

Life is full of **choices**, and I choose to live it the best way I can until God is ready for me. I desire to better myself. That includes losing weight. People always told me, *"It's just baby fat; it will go away,"* but it hasn't. I got bigger as I got older. I tried changing my eating habits, but I couldn't. At the time, I was surrounded by junk food, with the only "healthy" thing in the house being water. At school, my peers would say to me, *"You're pretty…but you're fat."* I would go home and cry because my weight added to my list of insecurities.

I also want to go to college to make not only myself happy, but my mama as well. I would love to hear her say she's proud of me because I'm doing something positive. When I have moments of self-talk, I remind myself there is so much I would like to do with my life, but I must be willing to make changes. I'm sure I can do it. Honestly, I haven't put much effort into doing so. I even want to make my daddy proud of his youngest child. I want to hear my sisters and brothers say, ***"I want the same mindset that you have, Shatoria!"*** I am determined to get myself together, even if it means taking baby steps to get there.

I have done so many things to fit in with others and to feel accepted. It's time for me to move past the things I've done and press forward. All the problems I've faced empower me and give me the courage to stand alone, now and in the future. Life is full of joys, pleasures, successes, and comfort…punctuated by misery, defeat, failures, and problems. At the age of 16, I now know I must walk my own path and prepare to adopt an adult mindset. As well, I have forgiven those who have hurt me. Forgiveness is the key!

When my mama told me about this *Teen Talk* book project, I hesitated at first. Two days later, I told her I would participate. I believe that with God, we **ALL** can overcome the obstacles on life's path. Whether we choose to accept it or not, there are pros and cons to **everything** we do. Let's step up and speak out so that we can help ***other*** teens do the same!

Supporting Cast Member Tamya Hibbler

Tamya Hibbler is a 16-year-old who was born on Christmas Eve. She's the only child from her mother's side. As a child, she always enjoyed reading. She loves going to church and praising God. She also likes going to the mall, dancing, and enjoying life. Tamya desires to one day work in the medical field.

ACCEPTANCE CAN BE DEADLY

A lot of you may have experienced peer pressure, but what exactly is it? **Peer pressure** is when you or a group of people are forced to do something by someone else that doesn't make you feel comfortable. For example, if you have a friend you've been friends with for years, then all of a sudden, that person may work to influence you to smoke weed when you know that's something you don't do—guess what? **Your peer has just pressured you!** The funny thing about peer pressure is that it doesn't end in our teens. Some adults do things they aren't comfortable doing, all because it's the "popular" thing to do.

Peer pressure can affect you in many ways. Teens fall into a trap, doing wrong things to be like others when they know that smoking, drinking, or whatever the case is wrong. They are negative influences. ***Why try to fit in, when there's nothing wrong with being yourself?*** I'm sure you were raised better than that! Plus, if you make the **wrong** choice, you can mess up your future, to include your education, career, and family.

I can't fail to mention that succumbing to peer pressure can affect your health. Cancers and a lack of overall good health are very real possibilities. Countless teens have **died** from drug overdoses, all because it was the "popular" thing to do. Or how about being pressured to jump into a pool, knowing you can't swim? **You could die!** Other things I've known teens to do just to be accepted were becoming an alcoholic, selling drugs, ditching school to smoke weed, and changing their attitude or behavior. Always remember: This is your life, not your friend's life. They may be working to make you be like them, just to make them happy.

A NOTE TO PARENTS: If you notice your child looks depressed or you see a change in them, talk to your child or get them some help right away. It's a sign that ***something*** is wrong.

Virtually every teen has an online presence on social media such as Snapchat, Instagram, Facebook, and Twitter *(to name a few)*. Peer pressure is commonplace on those sites as well. Before you know it, your self-esteem is low, and you are thinking negatively about yourself. Think about it: Most people only post their best pictures or are afraid to post images of the "real them" because social media has become so much about one's outer appearance. You must look **perfect**! That can make teens feel as if they're pressured online.

Most importantly, we must be cautious. Teens ages 14 – 18 who are on social media are often exposed to sex and the possibility of dating someone much older than them through deceptive practices of adults. It's not always cool to do what our peers are doing.

In this world today, there seems to be more of a need to "get in where you can fit in." Peer pressure is a way of effectively putting yourself through something you don't have to go through. Don't do things just to be popular. There's **nothing** wrong with having friends; we all need them. However, you should choose them wisely. Pick friends who are not going to pressure you to do things you don't want to do. Think about your life, what you have…and what you can lose—*including your **life***. If you feel like you are being pressured into doing things you don't want to do and know are wrong, pray and ask **God** to give you the strength to say "**NO!**"

As you continue to mature, I hope you will reflect on my story and allow it to help you make better decisions starting **TODAY!**

Supporting Cast Member
Tayler Wright-Williams

Tayler Wright-Williams is a 9-year-old Author and Youth Entrepreneur. She resides in Flint, Michigan, with her mother, Ms. Keywana Wright. Tayler is the creator of Tayler's Lip Balm, a homemade lip balm company that started with an idea for her school Science Fair. With the assistance of her mother, she wrote a book titled *I Like My Lip Balm* that is available for purchase online. Tayler enjoys playing video games, watching the Disney channel, dancing, and playing basketball. Her favorite food is chicken, her favorite colors are pink and purple, and her favorite subjects are Science and Math.

THE BULLYING STOPS WITH ME!

Have you ever experienced being bullied? I define bullying as a boy or girl saying something mean or hits and teases you. Webster's Dictionary defines bullying as *"one who intimidates those who are smaller or weaker."* It doesn't feel good to be bullied. Kids at my school have targeted me, and it has made me cry. I often talk to my grandmother about it. She listens and then tells my mother, who will then address the problem or concern with my teacher.

I remember the time some kids teased me about my tennis shoes. When I made it home, I cried and told my grandmother and mother I didn't like my shoes anymore. I then asked my mother to buy me a pair of Jordan's. After all, other kids had Jordan's, and they weren't being teased. My mother went right out and bought me a pair. The next day, the kids no longer teased me, which made me feel good. My mother explained that even though she bought me the shoes I asked for, I shouldn't let my peers make me feel bad about a pair of shoes *(before I was teased, I liked my other pair of shoes)*. She also told me I can have my own identity and shouldn't allow the opinions of others to change what I like.

In my school, the policy is that every student must wear the appropriate school uniform. My principal said we wear uniforms so that the kids will not focus on what they wear but will focus on learning. I like wearing uniforms to school because it stops people from picking on others because they're not wearing the latest style or brand-name clothes.

Another time I recall being bullied was when my hair was braided with added hair. One of my classmates asked me why I never wear my hair without the added hair. Another girl responded, *"Because she is bald-headed."* When I went home after school that day, I told my mother I didn't want to wear added hair in my hair anymore. When she asked me how I wanted to wear my hair, I replied, *"I want to wear my own hair"*—followed by a flood of tears.

My mother said, *"Let me tell you why I braid your hair. Your hair is long and healthy. I braid your hair so that it will stay long and healthy. The hairstyles you have are up-to-date and stylish. Most young girls and teens are wearing those styles."* After that conversation, I felt better. The next day at school,

I didn't let what the girls said the day before bother me.

There was another time when a girl kept hitting and pushing me at school. When it was time to line up to walk down the hallway, she would always go past me and hit or push me while I was standing in line. One day, I hit her back, and the teacher saw me. I got in trouble and was sent to the principal's office. I explained to the principal what happened, and even though the girl assaulted me first, my principal said, *"You shouldn't have hit her back. The next time she hits or pushes you, tell the teacher."* As a result of that incident, both of us were punished by having our gym time taken away.

My mother doesn't like it when I am picked on, and she will talk to my teacher about it. My mother says to me, *"I want you to be nice to other kids and play with the ones who are nice to you."* She often reminds me to avoid the mean ones. I must admit that it's hard sometimes because I want to make friends, play, and have fun. My mother and I often talk about the topic of bullies, and she tells me, *"Tayler, you can't let others change how you feel about yourself or something. It doesn't matter what others say."* I respond by telling her I am too young to understand what she's saying. I know she wants me to be a positive person and have my own identity...*whatever **THAT** means.*

****

Tayler's Mom Speaks

According to the online source Bullying.com, children between the ages of 9 - 11 are most common to be bullied or bully others. As Tayler's mother, I have always encouraged my daughter to **tell someone** if she is being bullied or having problems at school.

Recently, she shared with me that a girl in her class said she was "ugly and fat." I told her if the girl says that again, respond by saying, ***"I am beautiful. God made me the way I am."*** I believe it is vital that we encourage and tell our children they are special and important. I also think if they are told those things at home first, when they are faced with someone saying something mean to them, they will most likely think about what they have heard at home. Confidence-building should start at home.

In addition, the online source, "How to Build Children's Confidence" by Trudi Griffin, states *"children are sensitive and influenced by the world around them."* Children often look up to adults, who are their role models. Speak specific words of encouragement. It will help to boost the child's confidence!

As for me, I will continue to encourage my daughter by telling her she is smart, that she can do it *(whenever she has doubts),* and that she belongs. We speak those words of affirmation every day on the way to school. I firmly believe in the power of affirmations and speaking positive words into one's life.

It's Your Moment to SPEAK UP!

Use this time to write about whatever hardship(s) you are experiencing during your teen years. Then, share it with an adult you trust. Remember: That person has likely "been there and done that," so they can help you maneuver through whatever the circumstance.

CONCLUSION

You have arrived at the end of this book; **however**, the work for you is just beginning.

As you can see, the teen experience is one that is not a foreign concept…it's simply differs from one person to the next. What will you do differently starting **TODAY** that can make your future brighter? How can you be an influencer among your peers instead of a follower? Seriously think about your honest response to those two questions.

When seeking your real identity, know that mimicking others isn't ideal. It is said that standing alone can get lonely at times, but it is a necessity to avoid pitfalls. At this moment, consider who your friends are. Do they pressure you to be someone you know you're not **OR** do they realize your potential and uplift you with empowering words? There is a significant difference between friends and associates—primarily the *quality* of association determines the place those people hold in your life. It is better to be yourself and have no friends than to be like your friends and have no "self." Don't lower your standards to fit in or shrink who you are to make others comfortable. To please God, you may have to disappoint some people.

Never be embarrassed about your struggle. There is no shame in working hard to get to where you want to be. When nobody else celebrates you, learn to celebrate yourself! Put your focus into loving and creating, not gossiping and hating. If you are having a hard time right now, remember this: It's only temporary.

For the foreseeable future, this book will release annually with new teens and fresh perspectives on the teen experience. You are welcome to share **YOUR** story and help others along the way! Contact Pearly Gates Publishing using the information located at the end of this book to add your name to the list for upcoming projects. A member of our staff will contact you/your parent with more information.

Thank you for taking the time to read these encouraging stories written by teens for teens. Let's get the conversation going by discussing those issues addressed herein, in addition to your own. It's time to **SPEAK UP!**

ABOUT THE COMPILER

Angela R. Edwards is the CEO and Chief Editorial Director of Pearly Gates Publishing, LLC (PGP) and Redemption's Story Publishing, LLC (RSP)—Award-Winning International Christian Book Publishing Houses located in Houston, Texas. In May 2018, PGP was honored as the 2018 Winner of Distinction for Publishing in South Houston, Texas, by the Better Business Bureau (BBB). In 2019 and 2020, she was awarded

BBB Gold Star Certificates for both entities for her exemplary service to the community.

Angela's mantra is ***"My Words Have POWER!"*** Since its inception in January 2015, PGP has been blessed with an ever-growing and diverse group of almost 100 authors who have penned topics related to faith, love, abuse, bullying, Bible study tools, marriage, and so much more. Their youngest published author was only two years old; their eldest is 75 years old at the time of this publication. To their credit and God's glory, PGP and RSP have collectively over 150 best-selling titles to date.

An affordable publishing option (in comparison to some of the large, traditional publishing houses), PGP and RSP work one-on-one with authors to ensure that financial hardship is not a discouraging part of the publishing process. For those desiring to share their God-inspired messages for the masses, to include both new and 'seasoned' authors, both publishing houses provide unique services and support that many have said "left them feeling as if they are the only author" placed under each company's care.

The Holy Bible states that *"God loves a cheerful giver"* (2 Corinthians 9:7). To that end, PGP and RSP are frequently found hosting fantastic giveaways. Throughout the past few years, new author contests have awarded authors over $12,000 in services total.

In addition to the aforementioned, Angela is a domestic abuse survivor. Since first telling her abuse-survivor story publicly, she has become a 'Trumpet for Change.' She established the **"Battle-Scar Free Movement"**—an online community of individuals who freely express and share their own overcoming-testimonies. At the same time, they begin the very necessary healing process of the heart, mind, and soul. As part of her God-given mission, she provides abuse victims and survivors a **FREE** opportunity to anonymously share their testimonies in a book series entitled *God Says I am Battle-ScarFree.* Although the series will be completed in the Spring of 2021, Angela's mission to help individuals heal with the power of their words will continue. Assisting others with the healing process is paramount to her, which propelled her into becoming a volunteer Mentor for the Star of Hope Mission in Houston, Texas.

Angela holds an A.A. Degree in Business Administration from the University of Phoenix and is working towards her B.S. Degree in Psychology with a concentration in Christian Counseling from LeTourneau University. She is a woman of God, wife, mother, grandmother of 12, and a trusted friend. Originally a New Jersey native, she has since made Texas her home and embraced the southern culture in all of its fullness. She loves life and affirms daily: **"NOT TODAY, SATAN!"**

CONTACT THE PUBLISHER

Pearly Gates Publishing and Redemption's Story Publishing are always looking for new talent and desires to "birth the writer" in **YOU**! Will ***YOU*** be next on their list of ***Best-Selling Authors***?

Contact us today!

Visit PGP on the Web at
www.PearlyGatesPublishing.com

Visit RSP on the Web at
www.Redemptions-Story.com

Connect with PGP on Facebook at
facebook.com/pearlygatespublishing

Connect with RSP on Facebook at
facebook.com/RedemptionsStoryPublishing

Email Angela Edwards, CEO at
pearlygatespublishing@gmail.com

Call 832-994-8797
to schedule your **FREE** 15-minute publishing consultation.

www.ingramcontent.com/pod-product-compliance
Lightning Source LLC
Chambersburg PA
CBHW071213020426
42333CB00015B/1391
* 9 7 8 1 9 4 7 4 4 5 0 3 1 *